January 1985

Tricia - I hope your midlife crises are no more painful than most of mine — having a daughter like you surely helps.

Love you,
Mom

HOW TO SURVIVE YOUR HIGH SCHOOL REUNION... AND OTHER MID-LIFE CRISES

HOW TO SURVIVE YOUR HIGH SCHOOL REUNION... AND OTHER MID-LIFE CRISES

JUDY MARKEY

Contemporary Books, Inc.
Chicago

Library of Congress Cataloging in Publication Data

Markey, Judy.
    How to survive your high school reunion—and other mid-life crises.

    1. Middle aged women—United States—Psychology—
Anecdotes, facetiae, satire, etc.   2. Class reunions—
United States—Anecdotes, facetiae, satire, etc.
I. Title.
HQ1059.5.U5M37   1984   158'.0880564   84-11408
ISBN 0-8092-5380-1

Published by Contemporary Books, Inc.
180 North Michigan Avenue, Chicago, Illinois 60601
Manufactured in the United States of America
Library of Congress Catalog Card Number: 84-11408
International Standard Book Number: 0-8092-5380-1

Published simultaneously in Canada by Beaverbooks, Ltd.
195 Allstate Parkway, Valleywood Business Park
Markham, Ontario L3R 4T8 Canada

For Thomas—of course

CONTENTS

INTRODUCTION

The writing began a mere 16 years after graduation from journalism school. It took that long because at age 21 (a) I knew writing was torturously hard and (b) I wasn't sure I had anything to say. Only one of those things had changed by age 37—I finally had something to say.

That realization was not exactly the philosophical epiphany it may sound like. It came instead in the frozen food section at the supermarket. Our family had just moved back to America after six years as expatriates in Europe. I was trying to stock the shelves of our new, highly mortgaged kitchen and found myself overwhelmed with all the options (62 kinds of cereal, 14 versions of peas, 17 colors of hand soap) that everyone here took for granted. It wasn't that I'd forgotten how to say "milk" in my native tongue, but the plethora of nutritional alternatives truly did bemuse me. So I sat down at my Smith Corona and tried to explain how most of the world did not consider it normal to be able to purchase a sponge in the shape of a bologna sandwich.

The *Chicago Tribune* bought that first piece. I got a check in the mail, a picture in the paper, and a great excuse never to have to play tennis again. I could be a journalist. My mother always said so, but that didn't count. Mary Knoblauch at the *Tribune* said so—and that counted a lot. And within 18 months the byline had run in the *New York Times*, *Cosmopolitan*, *McCalls*, and *Savvy*.

Hey, this was fun. Not real lucrative, but a lot of fun. And gratifying. And the gratification came because of dreaded reason (a) cited above—it was hard. My head sometimes hurt at the end of the day. But I sort of liked that mental depletion, which was a whole lot different from the physical and emotional depletion of mommying, wifing, and house-managing.

The real challenge came in December of 1982. By that time all I wanted to do was to grow up to be a columnist. Carroll Stoner at the Chicago *Sun-Times* gave me that chance. She and Jean Adelsman and Jim Hoge handed me everything I needed—an extraordinarily fertile environment, a twice weekly space, and only unending support.

Most of this collection comes from those *Sun-Times* pieces. They cover the usual territory for amusement and despair: dads 'n' moms 'n' kids 'n' marriage 'n' divorce 'n' sex 'n' money 'n' thighs 'n' all the other stuff we have to slog through before we can get to wherever we all think we're going. Much as I'd like to fancy myself a philosopher king, I'd never be presumptuous enough to assume these pieces offer The Definitive Observation on All of the Above.

They are simply the voice of one garden-variety neurotic trying to find a nugget of truth in the nutsiness of it all. And if they make you laugh a bit, cry a bit, or think a bit, then I'll be real pleased.

PART I

HOW TO SURVIVE YOUR HIGH SCHOOL REUNION

They come up like clockwork. Every decade or demi-decade we are cordially invited to reimmerse ourselves in memory-laden yesteryear. One thing about invitations to high school reunions—they trigger very non-beige responses. Some people grow borderline feverish with excitement at the thought of reencountering former honeys, heroes, and just plain pals. (Of course, whether this enthusiasm is rooted in healthy or bitchy curiosity is not always evident.) However, there is a significant portion of the population adamant about avoiding reunions at all costs—the present apparently being so wonderful that the past becomes anathema. (Or perhaps it's merely that present-day malaise is infinitely preferable to that of the past.)

And it is predominantly to this sector, haters of high school memories, that this is addressed. For I too grew squinty-eyed and suspicious about the emotional and behavioral backlash I'd suffer by reexposing myself as an adult to that adolescent pecking order. I too was loathe to open that Pandora's box of pain. Masochism has never been my strong suit.

But inquisitiveness is. And that, combined with the fact that

I tend to be spineless under pressure from friends, is the sum total of the complex and noble motivations prompting my attendance at a gathering whose allure I'd historically viewed as only slightly less than that of my own funeral. To admit that I went, after years of oh-no-not-EVER speeches, is indeed humbling. But the next confession makes the preceding one benign. I HAD A WONDERFUL TIME. Beyond wonderful.

I went to a class reunion that transcended fun and segued directly into the arena of emotional luminescence. And at the risk of sounding like some born-again nostalgia freak, I'm convinced that anyone who even loosely adheres to the following 11-point program not only will survive the damn reunion, but will be forced to admit it was an exceedingly terrific place to put in an appearance.

1. When the invitation comes, and your trepidation threshold escalates, abandon all that knee-jerk negativism or should I/shouldn't I equivocation, and just GO.
Listen, all of us from first string cheerleaders to debate team drones are haunted by negative self-images of ourselves in high school. Self-imposed negative self-images. It was staggering to hear one of the top of the line class cuties admit she was terrified to go to the reunion and face those "boys" who always used to ignore her or were only nice to her in order to get dating access to her best friend. The person talking was a girl whose position on the rigidly defined popularity pyramid was coveted by 99.8 percent of the class. And yet all her old self-deprecation buttons were ready to be pushed when reunion time came around. So she wrestled with the pre-reunion push/pull and what she discovered was that showing up purged her of the residual icks she'd nurtured all those years.

Because all those boys who used to ignore her and all those girls whose intellect was so much more finely honed than hers, well they showed up, too. And it became evident that jagged, sullen, difficult adolescents had metamorphosed into wonderful adults. A veritable roomful of you're-not-getting-older-you're-getting-betters. And because they're better, wiser, kinder adults than 18-year-olds, ancient insecurities aren't re-ignited, they're dissipated. Zap.

And what you are left with is an immense sense of gratification and wonderment when you reencounter a rounded-out, seasoned version of a former classmate. For example: Guy Sanders. Guy Sanders was the Marlon Brando of the class— scowly, brawny, and very bright. He started to shave a shockingly handsome face in the seventh grade, and from that moment on, had every female's heart tied up in knots. But instead of parlaying his heartbreak potential to its maximum, Guy pulled back from our idolatry and grew rather isolated and aloof. Even though he drifted off with some of our ersatz intelligentsia, he remained for all of us an intensely magnetic presence. That's the background.

So how would you feel if a decade or so later a navy suited man with a mischievous mustache and crinkly dark eyes extends his hand toward you, and says, "Hey, hi. I'm Guy, do you remember me?" Remember you? We would have killed for a two-line conversation with you a few years ago. The inaccessibility evaporates, and standing in front of you, no longer brawny and assuredly grayer, is a lovely man looking something like a *mensch*-y Cesar Chavez telling you about life in the Napa Valley and showing you pictures of his wife and kids. Which brings up the next point. . . .

2. Bring no spouse; bring no date.
While the temptation is clearly to march in there with one swell male specimen by your side, corporal evidence that no matter how they remember you, someone now finds you cherishable, leave him home. You're a grown-up now—isn't that the point of this whole thing?

Even if the man in your life is a mogul of prominence or a Newman-Redford clone, be assured his presence will be less than enhancing. His presence will be classic third wheeldom. This is your night, your past, and this guy is going to feel like

Margaret Mead observing a group of people who share an obtuse background and undecipherable tribal connections. He will grow weary, if not hostile, watching you squeal and fall into the arms of someone he's never heard you mention. He will grow hurt by the obvious lack of interest people will show in him, while they are catching up on you. He will grow bored; he will grow sullen; he will probably grow drunk with the few other disgruntled demi-dyads. And it will only be a few that arrive in dyad form anyway. Your class probably isn't immune to national divorce statistics, so figure at least half those showing up will be in various unmatched stages of sequential spousedom.

In addition to the aforementioned altruistic rationale of protecting the man in your life from an evening of ennui, there is the practical matter to consider of protecting your own backside. More succinctly put: to the outsider, and that's what he'll be that night, your responses could seem to fall into the realm of the outrageous and asinine. Tears, laughter, confessions abound. You'll look like a participant in a Fellini extravaganza and it's very likely that when the show is over, he'll be unable to resist a few pointed observations. Could you, if you'd been relegated to the emotional bleachers all night? Best to avoid the potential of his playing snotty John Simon to your sentimental indulgences.

And lastly, there's the most obvious advantage of not attending a reunion smugly coupled: nostalgic sex (see point 10). Try as we may to rise above these things, the sexual encounter with one of your personal oldie-but-goodies becomes a real possibility if you can just screw (no pun intended) up the courage to tough it out at the reunion *toute seule*. Of course, a splendid alternative is to . . .

3. Go with an old class friend.
Even if you haven't been in touch for years and the last you heard was that she was on an alfalfa sprout commune in Colorado, call her parents and try to ferret her out. More than likely she's leveled off and has Visa bills and Pac-Man in her life now, too. And even if she doesn't, she's probably in the

throes of a to go/not to go quandary and between the two of you, you can probably muster enough communal courage to tread gingerly down memory lane.

The pluses of plunging into this time-warp fest with an old pal are many. Firstly, it will afford you an extended time to reconnect with someone who once meant a lot to you, and you'll avoid having to compress it all into the reunion itself. While you may be dubious that you'll have no more than ten minutes of mutuality to share with this person, what you'll probably discover instead qualifies as one of life's more humbling veracities: no matter how unique we feel ourselves to be—our hard-earned insights, our priorities, our angsts, our neuroses—the vicissitudes of life ultimately act as a certain leveler and what we perceive as being acutely idiosyn-cratic to ourselves ends up being yet one more pat categoriza-tion in Gail Sheehy's latest book. The point of all this being you will probably find enough in common with your old crony that it won't be a completely oil and water setup.

Secondly, it is enormous fun to recapture that pajama party mentality so crucial to preparations preceding and analyses postscripting the event itself. Only another woman with whom you shared your 17th summer is going to be able to assess whether or not (or care whether or not) Donna Jane Hornbacker actually had extensive plastic surgery during those intervening years or merely took cheekbone pills and grew into her nose. Only with her can you roar at the regressive indecisiveness that resurfaces during the ablutions and cosmetic applications of making ready for the event. Weighty deliberations between blue shadow and brown, bra and no bra, cannot help but underline that at that moment the combined maturity level of two otherwise perfectly nor-mal post-25-year-old females could not possibly exceed 15½. You borrow her lipstick, she your perfume, and you will be suffused with a cloying *déjà-vu* sensation that you have indeed replugged into a Sock Hop State of Mind. However, the temporary teenage panic clutching you dissipates once you both take a final look in the mirror and confirm that you just happen to look dazzling. That's because . . .

4. Body preparation begins several months ahead.
The day the invitation arrives is usually not one during which you are at your best. Frequently it is a day when your hair is seriously in need of washing, a herpes simplex adorns the corner of your mouth, and a rancid jogging suit is the only piece of apparel you own that no longer constricts. Obviously not the optimum look for a once-a-decade return engagement.

But what we have here is time—usually a couple of months—for salvaging the situation. In fact, it's this totally rigid time frame that makes it so easy to succeed. It's not like glancing waftily through *Vogue* and musing over someday svelteness and style. There's a concrete date, a major moment in which you'll be reencountered and recrystallized in the eyes of others, and you've got precisely X-number of weeks to refine the physical package you'll be presenting. Only Cinderella pulled it together in one night and you stopped believing in fairy godmothers years ago. This is your basic now-or-never deal, honey.

Resort to any shameful bribery or trickery to endure the hideousness of diet and the torture of exercise. I taped two photos to the refrigerator door: one curled and yellowed of me at my pert Sandra Dee best, terminally trapped in celluloid leading a silent cheer; the other, shamefully up-to-date and featuring a jiggly mother of two caught off-guard at a topless Club Med beach, an unfortunate confirmation of the old adage, "Old cheerleaders never die, but some parts give way. . . ." None of it hopeless, but all of it sorely in need of an overhaul.

Also, not to bog you down in the particulars of any one reunion, but mine was a California-based high school so a subliminal prerequisite of admission was to appear with at least a token tan. This was a somewhat tricky proposition, since in real life I abide in the heartland, approximately 1,500 miles from the nearest available ocean or desert. Our summer season tends not to exceed the regulation three months, and by Labor Day leaves are already crunching underfoot. Our reunion was the last weekend in September, and there was no way to extend my copper tones for an additional month, unless I wanted to expose my body to the odious ultra-rays of a Forever Tan franchise and spend hard-earned money for the pleasure of risking cancer. I actually reflected several days upon this, and being a woman of substantive values and a woman impervious to the superficial, made the obvious decision. I bared my face and body to potential noxious side effects and epidermal disaster in the name of Instant and Artificial Tan. I am not proud of this, but retell it as an illustration of how far one must be willing to go. One of my dear friends actually considered flying in from Austria for the reunion, but had to cancel at the last minute. Her nails just weren't long enough.

But presuming your alma mater has less stringent standards, it is entirely possible to pull yourself into certifiably grand-entrance shape within this fixed period. Maximum effort will yield maximum results. Just cross your fingers and hope that at the 11th hour Mother Nature doesn't sideswipe you with a pre-prom pimple. Commensurate with your efforts to prepare yourself physically, it is very important to . . .

5. Begin to prepare yourself mentally.
This takes place on two levels. The first is informational and basically a piece of cake. Not much required here, a bit of preliminary browsing through the yearbook in an attempt to ignite the flame of recognition of long forgotten names and faces. You should know that in spite of this pre-event prep course, a conversation may take place that night with your eyes glued on the nametag of, not the face of, a person who regales you with vivid anecdotes of the intimate times spent together while you try valiantly to figure out who the hell he or she was. (Lest you get unduly flattered about your apparent import to a nonentity, the syndrome kicks into reverse and there will probably be someone very confused about your identity as you confide how one of your major thrills was sitting next to him in sophomore study hall.) Nevertheless, dust off your Clarion and dredge up some of those dusty names and faces that memory has long repressed.

❧ The second level is attitudinal, and while it is much trickier to master, it is pivotal if you are to avoid some potentially poisonous pre-reunion mind sets:

a) *Gleeful curiosity about what the ravages of time have done to former prom queens and football captains.* Do not rub your hands together in anticipation of disaster. These types are frequently well preserved and in the long run you will probably find this soothing. Collapsed queens tend to be a depressing sight—tangible testimony to the transitory nature of beauty and all that. Better to leave those revelations to the poets than be confronted with the blowzy, bodily evidence of some poor dear who peaked at 17.

b) *The I'll-Show-Them Syndrome.* Granted, this is an especially tempting posture for people who spent their salad days as nonentities and who are now anchorwomen, or lieutenant governors, or even minor artists or major interior decorators. However, consider this caveat. If you are indeed hot stuff, most people will be cognizant of this and will approach you warily on the assumption that fame and recognition have likely tarnished the unassuming person you once were. They may presume you are going to be uppity, and should your demeanor confirm that, they will be poised and ready to lump you into the old Will-Success-Spoil-Rock-Hunter? syndrome. Adopting an attitude of accessibility and good-ole-girlness would be a much more satisfying stance.

c) *The I Was Voted "Most Likely to Succeed" and Still Haven't Been on The Donahue Show Despair.* This is of course the flip side of the above. You were the class officer and exchange student and the only one to go to a prestigious eastern school. These people pinned their hopes on you and expected great and thunderous life moves. *Quelle* letdown. You still live eight blocks from school, are a little bit estranged from your second husband, and are working part-time as a secretary for an insurance company. You did have two short stories published in *The New Yorker* some years ago, but it's going to be a bit of a stretch steering the conversation around to that. You have been battered by life's vagaries and are convinced that appearing in this condition will trigger either gloating or depression among your former classmates. Best not to dwell on any of this. Instead rest assured that you will not be the only victim of real life's *sturm und drang*, and muster up the remnants of your former buoyancy. By simply showing up they'll know you're a survivor.

d) *You were the class bitch, or bookworm, or black sheep, and they'll never let you forget it.* This is a common gnawing fear, but one that is seldom justified. At age 27, after several years of therapy, one of the class glamoratti realized that she spent much of her youth being an appallingly snotty human being. She cringed retroactively and, swamped with an aversion to ever return to the scene of her heinous crimes, couldn't face being a participant in the reunion proceedings. She was much missed, even by some of us who were her most battered victims. (Teenage transgressions pale considerably in light of the more recent violations we frequently endure.) Not only will your classmates grant you absolution, but you may find yourself in the ironic position of being honored for the very acts and attitudes that once ostracized you—as in the inspirational Renee Stillwater Story. Renee was our raciest, bawdiest, most scarlet of ladies. Rumor had it that her absence at graduation wasn't linked to deficient grades but to deficient birth control protection. It no doubt took great courage to return, but then she was treated to a moment of exquisite, albeit Pyrrhic victory. Renee Stillwater received a case of champagne for being the class member with the oldest and the most children.

e) *The unfinished business of unrequited sex.* (Unrequited sex being rather prevalent until the late '60s, when requited sex became a bit more fashionable.) Without question, this is the most tempting and the most perilous expectation to nurture. Everyone is haunted by the we-did-everything-

but boy in their life. Everyone remembers all the wrenching you-would-if-you-really-loved-me harangues con-
ducted in the rec rooms and backseats of cars. And everyone, fatigued and jaded by the sexual license of recent
years, yearns to recapture the intensity of those urges we
suppressed in the name of Holding Out. We all have old
sexual scores to settle, but going to the reunion primed for
the kill almost guarantees disaster. What makes this different from nostalgic sex (see point 10) is that this is founded
on *premeditation.* You not only run the risk that
paunches and encroaching baldness will render your
former lust object unrecognizable, but like anything you
gear up for with fierce determination, you increase your
chances for vast disappointment. And there's no place
quite so devastating as the sexual arena in which to have
an anti-climax. Healthy curiosity about past paramours is
permissible, but trying to orchestrate grand finales to
romantic dramas played out years ago is likely to be a
doomed endeavor.

**6. Be artful, and not too deceitful, with the information you
submit to the Class Reunion Souvenir Book.**
Remember that the data you send in will define you in black
and white for the next ten years. You want to be impressive,
but brisk—none of these endless titles like "Northeastern
Manager for Personnel Training and Career Management for
the McCormick-Howard Shoe Lace Company." On the other
hand, you don't want to be too generic and just say "chicken
business." You want something succinct—yet panoramic;
socko—yet incorporating your many facets. I think the most
masterful listing from our souvenir book, and truly reflective
of the chameleon-like California citizenry, was the following:
"Jeannie Frampton—psychiatric social worker/casting direc-
tor." Need one say more?

Although in high school we channeled our energies into
being just like everybody else, these souvenir books bear remarkable testimony to the wondrously helter-skelter paths

we've taken as grown-ups. Neurosurgeons and judges are on the same pages as demolition experts, pastors, and exotic dancers. There's a splendid Breughelian scope to these books in spite of there being something of a statistical preponderance of one profession or another, depending on your alma mater. (Mine being an L.A. class, perhaps 40 percent wound up as shrinks; my husband's being a Cleveland class, perhaps 40 percent wound up as podiatrists.)

What you should shoot for here is presenting the general truth with clout and flair. Instead of desolately labeling yourself as "housewife," you could say: "cookbook author" (you sent in six ideas for "The PTA Recipe Book," didn't you?); "studying law" (these progressive tense verbs offer terrific latitude); "domestic consultant" (which merely means people often ask you "where did you get those great knickers," "how did you handle it when he made a pass at you," or "who is your gynecologist?").

Creative biographical information completed, the next item on the agenda is . . .

7. The Outfit.
Choose something that is sartorially definitive of the woman you've become. Because you are no doubt multi-faceted, this can present something of a quandary, but select a facet and go with it. Since adolescents of my vintage were generally decked out in prehistoric preppy, many had by now wearied of Peter Pan collars, and the predominant look at our reunion was pure vamp. The room was rife with cleavage.

But there are also myriad variations. Remember, it's not the style you choose, it's choosing to do it with style. (Did anyone really ever say that?) The biggest knockouts are frequently former ugly ducklings, who years ago couldn't cram into our rigid definition of Gidgetian cute. These once gawky, frizzy-haired outcasts seem to have turned the tables on capricious Mother Nature and slink back to the reunion lithe and dramatic as hell. Imagine Cher in high school.

For this night, it's just not enough to be presentable. The

object is to galvanize them. The possibilities are endless—whether it's a great-looking silk suit, a wafty caftan, a chic little black thing reeking of Good Taste, or a slinky jumpsuit, pull together something that makes you feel invincibly great. Because on that night, you're definitely going to need it. The butterflies will be careening through your innards, and while your eyes will tell you you look certifiably splendid, your viscera will be telling you this entire idea was sheer idiocy; but . . .

8. Take heart; also take your family photos and your business cards.

It may sound corny, but peppered through the evening will be requests by people to see your family pictures. Though they are genuinely interested, they're even more interested in your asking the same of them. And rest assured, they've come prepared. By evening's end you will be surfeited of snapshot repartee. But it's a standby reunion icebreaker, and there is something sensational about seeing former ruffians grow misty-eyed over smudgy little photos of their bucktoothed and bespectacled progeny. Aren't they darling? So, you lie a little. It's just a major reunion ritual, like the frenzied exchange of business cards. Why owners of craft 'n candle boutiques press their cards into the hands of tire distributors is never entirely clear, but it probably has little to do with commerce and more to do with (1) meaning well or (2) running out of conversation. Which brings us to the heart of the matter. . . .

9. Conversational dos and don'ts.

a) *Don't obsessively announce how you've changed and/or were misunderstood.* Evidence of this should be subtly suffused through your demeanor, not through declarations. An example: Robbie was the son of a notorious Las Vegas gangster who met an untimely demise. Our teenage penchant for typecasting no doubt meant he had little choice but to take on the role of head hood. (Which at the time meant he developed a great lip curl, got caught for smoking a lot, and combed his hair 80 times per class period.) Robbie hit everyone at the reunion with the same opener: "Hey, I was really a nice guy. How come you thought I was just a greaser?" It's difficult to work up a graceful response to that, especially if you are haunted by the possibility that he has indeed followed in his father's footsteps, and if you don't answer the question right, there could be serious bodily harm done to you or your loved ones. Of course, what you discover after spending a few minutes with him is that churlishness has given way to chivalry. Robbie actually pulls out a chair for you, settles you in, hands you a glass of wine, and is terribly dear and charming. He probably *was* misunderstood, but you would have figured it out without benefit of that awkward announcement.

b) *Don't try to overimpress; it backfires.* "So Joan, what are you doing these days?" "Well, I'm something of a wheel over at CBS." This is a direct quote from a woman who, up until that moment, I was really excited to see. A certain amount of self-effacement goes a long way to greasing the gears of social intercourse. This is not the same as false humility, but it does mean low-keying your way into any impressive credits you may feel bear mentioning. What you want to be giving off is a sense of your *serenity*, not your *success* (the former being a hell of a lot more elusive and enviable than the latter).

c) *Don't make the direct inquiry "Are you married?"* With all the marital disasters out there, and everyone in various stages of regrouping their domestic debris, this query could trigger some jagged responses. Better to couch it in the softer, albeit synthetic, phraseology "Do you have a family?" This tends to discourage lurid tales of matrimony gone awry and to expand the possible arena of response.*

---

*However, it does not expand it quite wide enough to include the gays. (Oh God, the complexities of social amenities in the '80s. Perhaps "Are you now, or have you ever been, involved in a meaningful relationship with a person of the same or opposite sex?" would cover it. . . .)

d) *Don't get bogged down with the class schizoid.* There will be at least one. Not necessarily the person you might have predicted would take up the mantle of mental imbalance, but these years have been hard. And whether it's hard drugs or the even harder knocks of life, rest assured there will be a certifiable wacko drifting through. Best to extricate yourself from meaningful conversations with this one.

e) *Don't overextend yourself alcoholically or ingest undue amounts of illegal substances.* This advice isn't predicated on a strong sense of morality, but rather on the observation that the most extraordinary highs to be obtained will come from partaking in and observing the combustive giddiness that occurs when all these people are reconnecting. If you are blitzed out on something, you'll miss all the noteworthy vignettes unfolding around you . . . like the reunion of two men once known as Fastball Eddie and The Muffler. As youths these fellows spent the major segment of their waking hours balancing full packs of Pall Malls in the rolled sleeves of their T-shirts. Vocabularies seldom exceeded grunt level and emotional displays were tightly circumscribed by the prevailing mores of staying, at all costs, cool. Ten or 20 years later they are tearfully locked in a euphoric embrace. "Jeez, I don't believe this." "God, this is incredible. . . ." Quite clearly their verbal and emotional vocabularies have somewhat expanded. It's scenarios like that, tugging on your heartstrings more than a "Little House on the Prairie" special, that you won't want to miss.

f) *Do be lavish with deceitful exclamations like "You haven't changed at all!"* Everybody's changed, but they'll appreciate your pretending they're still all dewy-eyed and taut. For those in whom change has been especially obvious but unkind, the above falsehood may stick in your gullet. In these cases, "It's really terrific to see you" can serve as an all-purpose exclamation. (Of course the ultimate accolade can be the reverse—"My God, you've changed!" It depends on the original point of reference, as in "My God you've changed, you used to be so plain, so fat, so etc.") "You look wonderful!" will also be bantered about with the sincerity usually reserved for used car salesmen and politicians, but don't be judicious in your use of these lies we love to hear. No one goes to these things hoping to be told that he looks like hell.

g) *Do seek out people peripheral to your high school experience, but pivotal to the preceding years.* These are people whose paths diverged so radically from yours in adolescence that by graduation you'd already quashed the memory that the first nine years of your lives were interwoven in the primitive power struggles played out daily on every kid's block. Ferret out little Howie who always wore brown suspenders or pathetic Mary Beth, whose mother always made her wear kneesocks, an offense for which she was tortured mercilessly. It's odd how seeing these people from the scruffy-kneed segment of your past renders you a quavery mass of sentimental jello. These are the people who were privy to the primal you—the one you've been trying to unearth after all these years on the couch. These are the people who frequently provide not only the most touching encounters, but some of the most revelatory. "You mean you don't remember when you organized everyone for the block-wide 'doctor olympics' and I kept having to be the patient? You were the meanest, bossiest little girl I ever knew. . . ." A few rancorless recollections like that and it might be exceedingly difficult to wait until Monday to see the shrink.

h) *Do demystify old demons.* This is your chance to walk up to those who formerly intimidated you or who immobilized you with the most humiliating strains of love sickness and 'fess up. The advantage of this are many. (1) It gives you an excuse to talk to them. (2) It may momentarily embarrass them, but it will undoubtedly make them purr with retroactive pleasure. (3) It is a singular moment to purge yourself of those haunting memories of Great Moments in Adolescent Assholedom. (4) It gives you the occasion to uncover whether these formerly awesome presences are indeed an accessible, interesting human beings, total wipeouts, or fall somewhere in between. In any case, you'll no longer cringe with shame or envy or wrenching palpitations if their names are mentioned or they make guest appearances in a dream of yours. And you'll have made great breakthroughs in dismantling the mystique in which you creatively enveloped them and which frequently elevated C- characters into venerated personages.

The technique you employ for demystification can be flexible. It's not necessary to confront someone with toe-curling candor: "Did you know I always wanted to (fill in the blank) with you?" It's possible to sidle in on these things by subtly couching your confessional statement in insouciance: You toss your head back in a throaty laugh, mist your eyes over with manufactured sophistication, lean forward conspiratorially as you touch his arm, and then whisper, "Did you know I always wanted to (fill in the blank) with you?" Gets 'em every time. Sometimes it even gets you more than you'd bargained for. . . .

10. Nostalgic Sex.

It is indeed true that the preceding "conversational do" can lead to what we have come to refer to as Nostalgic Sex. But as stated in item 5e, Nostalgic Sex falls far afield of the obsessing and plotting to act out your musty old fantasies. Nostalgic Sex only blossoms in an environment of spontaneity, of caprice, which is of course what makes it such a singularly shimmery event. A typical Nostalgic Sex scenario unfolds thusly: An old beau, but not necessarily *the* old beau, shows up at the reunion. You've had no news of or contact with him for more years than are countable, and confronting you is a divorced high school coach with a son nearly as old as he had been when last you tussled through the regulation petting ballets of your one semester as steadies. You discover that you have enough in common for more than a 15-minute catch-up conversation so you go out after the reunion and spend the next four hours uncovering how each other thinks and feels and lives as grown-ups. It becomes apparent that you like each other as grown-ups, and that there are still stirrings of a sort of affectionate chemistry between you. What follows is absolutely outrageous, great fun, and very tender. There have doubtless been times in your life when you've done it for passion, done it for mercy, done it for power, or done it for duty, but there's nothing quite like doing it for nostalgia. It is something of an ephemeral, bittersweet carnal coda on the evening's events. You will marvel at the grandness of it, the no-strings-ness of it, its total exemption from what we frequently allude to as Real Life. Nostalgic Sex is not a thing to be sought, but it's definitely a thing to be savored. However, should it not be in the cards for you that night . . .

11. Do find a group of people to leave with.
You'll want to synthesize all the unfocused observations and feelings triggered during the last few hours, a difficult task to undertake alone. By getting a small group together, delicious crosscurrents of gossip will emerge and coalesce to either validate or explode impressions you picked up during the evening—a kind of Rashomon review of the proceedings. It's not only enhancing, it's cathartic. Several of us—I think we numbered a jury-like 12, all from disparate nooks and crannies of the once clearly delineated social strata—found ourselves bound together by a post-reunion need to nail some things down: inane things (who looked the youngest); sad things (how death came to classmates remembered as so invincible); mean-spirited things (now that she's famous, she's disclaimed knowing us all). But all of us bound together by an immense pride that the Archie and Veronica caricatures we once were had filled in and dimensionalized into rather accomplished thinking/feeling/ articulate adults. All of us bask-

ing in the evanescence of communal contentment—my God, we turned out OK after all. It's borderline miraculous when you think about it. All of us a bit quavery from the unexpectedly gratifying aspects of being together and all of us convinced that it's true: nostalgia isn't what it used to be. It's a whole lot better.

PART II

...AND OTHER MID-LIFE CRISES

1.

GROWING OLDER GRACEFULLY OR GRUDGINGLY
(TAKE YOUR PICK)

THE YOUNGER MAN: CAN YOU FOLLOW IN MTM'S *TOE* STEPS?

Item: Married—Mary Tyler Moore, 45, and Manhattan cardiologist Robert Levine, 31.

All those poor Mindy Morgensterns—28, bright, attractive, still mired in tautness and nubility—those Mindy Morgensterns never had a chance. Not when the likes of Dr. Robert Levine was fair game for one of us . . . older women. We *femmes d'un certain age* (the French say these things so well) are clearly becoming a force to be reckoned with in the old romantic arena.

Somewhere between the gigolos of *The Roman Spring of Mrs. Stone* and the predatory vamping of Mrs. Robinson in *The Graduate*, older women/younger men liaisoning acquired *un certain* fashionability. And now with everybody's favorite Mary ("well, gee, Mr. Grant") Richards leaping into the May/September breach, the syndrome has gained *un certain* legitimacy that even Burt and Dinah (remember?) never brought it.

The best part is that MTM's spouse/consort is nothing less than the Ultimate Good Catch in Real Life—a Jewish doctor. Granted, MTM isn't exactly Real Life—she's famous and she's

25

thin—but look at the major portion of 35-plus female people these days. I'm not talking the Evans/Fonda/ Steinem contingency, but the ones in your office or on your block. We do not look the way our mothers did at 40. More important, we do not feel the way our mothers did at 40. The middle is no longer the last pre-senility season before the big wind-down; the middle is a jumping-off point to about a zillion new beginnings and immense possibilities.

Not to mention hormones. We are talking serious, statistically documented sexual peaks here. We are talking lust without limits, ripeness without repression—after all, we've had several decades' experience surviving life's warpy little indignities, and that tends to leave us virtually unshockable in any domain, whether horizontal or vertical. We've broken through our mothers' girdle-and-seamed-stocking sexual teachings; we've gleaned what was useful from Germaine and Kate; our biological-clock dilemmas were resolved years ago, and we've even gotten over being angry that we wasted our youth chasing hollow myths.

A lot of that emotional wrenching is behind us, and unlike the Mindy Morgensterns—who are stressed out over making their MBAs pay off, locating their G-spots, and evaluating the merits of non-, single, or joint parenthood—we don't have to decide or prove anything by our next birthday. We are at a splendid point where we are biologically juiced up and emotionally calmed down. What a deal. How can the Dr. Levines of the world resist?

But what's in it for us? Aside from the obvious things, like flat bellies and having our attractiveness reconfirmed, what elevates this from its former implication of being a rash connection with a callow male to being a respectable connection with a credible male? All kinds of things.

- Statistics. A hefty percentage of the over-40 male population is divorced. And they frequently suffer a much slower and more incomplete recovery rate than the women they divorced. Which means a major portion of

the mature males feel pretty battered by, and not too crazy about, mature women. Younger men aren't angry.
- Power. The two traditional power bases in a relationship—being older and being male—are reduced by half. And anyway, younger men are more accustomed to parity, rather than power, with females.
- Comfort and creativity. Unfair as it is—older women probably have only the Mindy Morgensterns to thank for this—younger men are notoriously comfortable and creative with females. Younger men do everything. It is said they even do toes. *Toes.*

So 45 today is a whole lot different than it used to be. I bet when MTM's mother was 45, she wore sensible shoes. And now there's her daughter, getting twice-weekly pedicures.

⁕

WHEN IT'S EASIER TO BE NAKED THAN IN A BATHING SUIT

⁕

Your 40th birthday is days away. You're managing to remain at least moderately balanced about it. And then the editors of *Sports Illustrated* nail you. Their annual swimsuit issue hits the stands. And your tenuous hold on the you're-not-getting-older, you're-getting-better philosophy of life bites the dust. Better? You may be better in bed, you may be better in business, but better in a bathing suit? Not a chance.

There probably aren't 11 people on the face of this earth who look better in a bathing suit than the girls in *Sports Illustrated* and surely none of the 11 is a woman about to step into the fifth decade of her life.

Bathing suits and body anguish have always gone hand in hand. Body anguish is one of those things about-to-be-40 people work diligently to combat. A person of 40 has credibility and substance and character. A person of 40 also has jiggly upper arms and must labor valiantly to convince herself that substance counts more that sleekness. It's just easier to stay convinced when you're swaddled in a poncho than when you're spilling out of a bathing suit.

The current bathing suits are very hostile little garments. Just when you need it most, absolutely no support is being given to you. Not a whalebone, not an inner lining, not a bias cut in the bunch. Oh, these are cruel little numbers, purporting modesty because they are predominantly one piece, and yet exposing vast expanses of potentially corrugated flank and bottom. No one looks terrific in these bathing suits except a seriously thin person who is heavily into depilatories.

Of course, bathing suits always have been problematic because bathing-suit wearing always has been based on a faulty premise—that it's OK to be almost naked in a public place in broad daylight. Wrong, wrong, wrong. Not morally wrong, but psychologically wrong.

Very few of us, no matter what our age, are ever quite at peace with our bodily selves. So to have to unveil that body and to have to pretend that you are calm about complete strangers being able to see and judge that body is very distressing indeed.

It is easier to be naked than to be in a bathing suit. When you're naked, you're usually with someone who likes you a lot, so you probably will be forgiven for having a pair of thighs that are, ahem, Rubenesque. Corporal abundance in a one-on-one naked situation can even have an up side because often something nice and affectionate is said about there being more of you to love. But no way are there allowances for abundances displayed in a bathing suit.

Additionally, one-on-one nakedness almost never takes place in raw daylight. Even those brazen folks who make love with the lights on probably don't perform under anything more glaring than 40 watts. But bathing suits must be worn under the unforgiving sun and there are few thighs on earth that don't look a touch too dimpled under that harsh illumination.

Of all the clothes you buy, bathing suits are the one item that never enhance you—they just consistently embarrass you.

But look at it this way. Even though you're 40 and will feel real self-conscious on the beach, it still will be better than when you were 14 and feeling real self-conscious on the beach. At least when you dive into the surf now, no foam-rubber falsies will float to the surface in front of the entire sophomore class.

You'll take varicose veins and grown-up humiliation any day.

⁂

MENOPAUSAL BABY HAVING

⁂

Are you ready for this, folks? Here's another medical first to send shivers of wonderment down your spine: menopausal baby-having. Yes, indeed. Though menopause and babies once were considered mutually exclusive phenomena, good old modern science has figured out a way to merge them and circumvent Ma Nature yet another time. It would seem that the wisdom of this is dubious at best.

I think it's pretty appalling that these doctors progesteronized, then test-tube-embryoized, a slew of matronly monkeys, who had put in their kid-rearing time already, had survived years of experimental torment, and probably were looking forward to retirement at some Florida or Arizona laboratory. How would you feel if you were ready to pack your bags for

Sun City and then all of a sudden you got knocked up? Whammo. It is the ultimate "Go to Jail/Do Not Pass Go" Monopoly moment in life. Bad enough for a baboon to draw that card, but a real live woman? Why on earth would she even want to play the game?

This, I know, is a rather un-American statement to make, but not all well-balanced and moderately nurturing women melt, ipso facto, at the sight of a blanket-swaddled infant. We do not all look with envy upon the drooling cherubs toted in backpacks or scrunched into supermarket carts. The sight of juicy Gerber baby cheeks (be they face or bottom) does not send all of us into paroxysms of pinching. This doesn't mean we are highly aberrant. This only means we are highly aware.

Aware that babies are very troublesome creatures indeed. They inside-out your life in a way that prevents it from getting normal for a minimum of two decades. They are very demanding. And very messy. They are bald, conversationally invalid, their manners are atrocious, and they defile your wardrobe. Keeping them clean and fed is a thankless task centered on the endless shoveling in and mopping up of questionable substances in putrid colors. Fact is, there is a major portion of American womanhood that is nothing short of delighted that their baby-bearing days are a thing of their biological, chronological, and psychological past. I just can't understand why a woman in the mellowness of menopausal maturity would want to take two giant steps backward into the muck of motherhood.

Rejuvenation? Seeing the world again through the little nipper's eyes? Come on. The woman who craves rejuvenation surely would feel younger after some plastic surgery than she would after a stint of second-time-around sandbox sitting.

To please the young lifeguard in her life? The mid-life woman who has hooked up with her real-people Richard Gere is surely sage enough to realize that additional varicosities and stretch marks are not major enhancements to a person already on the far side of 40. It's hard to imagine that bambino-having would be particularly helpful in wonderfulizing one of these fashionable May/December relationships.

To plunge into a much-delayed "I've-Always-Wanted-a-Child" phase? It's difficult to fathom that a woman who has spent nearly half a century without benefit of tykes careening around her premises could, at this point in her life, say a permanent "so long" to closets full of silk blouses, pastel rooms redolent with serenity and fingerprintless mirrors, and leap directly and joyfully into the terminal chaos and crud that accompany the little critters.

It seems to me, once you hit your fabulous 50s, you would like a little fabulous in your life. Granted, fabulous comes in many formats, but when my reproductive system goes into retirement, I don't intend to be behind a stroller any more than I intend to be behind a walker.

I wish those scientists had talked to me first. Maybe then they'd have spent less time working on geriatric motherhood and more time on curing the common cold.

∗⁂∗

WHEN THE TRUTH OF 40 STRIKES
∗⁂∗

Still safely ensconced in my 39th year, I made many "this-is-the-best-time-in-our-lives" speeches to females to the right and left of me going through the tumult of turning 40. Bolstered by articles on Ali, Candice, Jane, and all the other just-like-you-and-me-but-still-looking-fabulous women, I waxed rhapsodic about the benefits of being birthed four instead of two or three decades ago. I was wise, I was seasoned, I was enlightened. I was full of it.

This came to me in an acutely painful flash recently when I realized that part of me would have traded it all to be eternally callow and taut. This humiliating admission came

about after vacationing in one of the most bizarre environ-
ments I've ever encountered—a Club Med.

Club Meds have a partially deserved reputation for being a
haven for horny singles. One reason is that they are set up
along the lines of a jazzy camp, with a large population of
counselors whose hiring is based on two main criteria—
being bilingual and being (especially in the case of the men)
sinfully smashing to look at. A regular guy from Chicago has
a hard time getting lucky there—it's a veritable village of
Adonises whose job descriptions include guest-romancing.

So married mid-lifers like me at the Club Med feel a bit
Margaret Meadian, observing, but not partaking in, the noctur-
nal rites of body rubbing and one-night stands. My initial
posture as part of a *fait-accompli* couple was laced with
amusement, indifference, and no small bit of smugness that I
was exempt from all the frenetic flirtation.

I assumed that after all those years on the couch, my
predilection for coquetry had been leached out. Wasn't I at 40
delighted to be a well-grounded woman whose sense of self
was rooted in her substantive rather than her seductive
assets? Apparently not. This depressing insight came to me
courtesy of a beyond-beautiful young man with one of those
wonderful hyphenated French names who sought nothing
more lustful than conversation with me, and with whom, to
my husband's great amusement, I became shamefully smitten.

He clearly was several echelons above the prevalent flexed-
pec lifeguard mentality of his co-workers, removed himself
from the disco-gigolo aspects of his job, and seemed to be a
genuinely graceful, thoughtful human being. I liked him as a
person, he liked me as a person, but seduced by all the
surrounding seductions, I became aware that I wanted him to
like me as a woman.

And that was an appalling realization. Appalling because I
have a historical horror of chronic vamps, Mrs. Robinsoning
their way into their twilight years. It all gets so increasingly
inappropriate.

But there I was having fantasies about serendipitously running into a 23-year-old sailing instructor a few years further into his adulthood when the chronological gap would be less acute, and he would be 30, and I'd be, oh my God, 47. Unless I decide to spend the next seven years shuttling between Nautilus and the plastic surgeon, I expect that by 47 my allure level will be but a faded blip on the screen of life. And that devastates me—not only that it will be gone, but that I mind so damn much.

My whole "it's-great-to-be-40" speech was rooted in the conviction that since we have so much more to offer now, we finally are liberated from needing to feel physically appealing. But I wonder if it ever really goes away. And I wonder if we won't all be 70-year-old Barbara Stanwycks futilely railing at the decades-younger Father de Bricassart in *The Thorn Birds*, "I have loved you. Inside this stupid body I'm still young, I still feel, I still want, I still dream." What a speech.

I think it might be a whole lot closer to the truth than the one I've been issuing. And that makes me tremble with despair because now I know that behind my sensible shoes and salt-and-pepper-bun facade, there will still be a Nastassia Kinski clawing to get out.

※

THE LAST OF
THE BLUE-HAIRED MAMAS

※

I worry about it a lot. Where are our future blue-haired ladies going to come from? It's true, you know; their ranks have dwindled until the blue-haired populace borders precariously on endangered species levels. And the reason for the dismal future of the azure-tressed? A profound resistance on the part of 87 percent of American women to growing older with a modicum of grace. We just can't do it. It goes against (you should pardon the expression) our culture.

I first noticed this several years ago while living in Rome. Italy is a country where "Mama" still means something serious, and respected, and the implication of maturity is not considered detrimental.

There a Mama looked like a Mama. Specifically that meant one of two things: (a) she wore at all times a black dress or (b) (and this was most often the case) she wore pearls and something subdued, but stylish, and her hair was swept back in some sort of classical salt-and-pepper swirl.

In the face of Grannydom in America, it was a reassuring sight.

Grannydom in America is, as we know, up for grabs. When our granny gets off the plane for her biannual visits, we take pre-arrival bets as to whether we'll be greeting a blond, a brunette, or a redhead. Her hand luggage does not contain toll house cookies in tins, pot roast in tupperware, or the latest copy of *Reader's Digest*. Her hand luggage contains only one sleek metal tennis racket and a copy of *Nice Girls Do*. When she unpacks there are no sensible shoes or print dresses in sight—there are instead sneakers and Calvins and jumpsuits that say "Funky Granny" on the back. Granny does not crochet or play duplicate. She is instead an avid aerobic dancer with Travoltaesque routines to all the latest records and she's going to night school to get her M.B.A.

Now wait. The above cataloguing is not intended to cast aspersion on the pursuit of youth or of maintaining an *au courant* mentality. In a way, who can argue with the swell-ness of that? How many of us had grannies who could take us on for two sets or discuss the latest findings of Shere Hite? It seems fine and even healthy for ladies who *expected* they'd feel old at 65 to discover those feelings are not obligatory.

But it's us Future Grannies of America I'm really worried about. We *don't expect* to feel old at 65; in fact we don't expect to *ever* feel old, or look old, or (God forbid) act old. How many of us 32-plus-year-olds still refer to our parents' friends as "the grown-ups"? Growing up seems so remote and improbable. After all, we still keep having these recurring bouts with acne to reassure us that we are indeed hormonally only 17. Sporadic acne and a few gray hairs—the irresistible combination of a woman in her sexual prime.

One thing about primes—one just hates to be on the down side of them. So the temptation is to try to extend this out into decades. I am especially haunted by the vision of my future granddaughter's date waiting in the living room 40 years hence. I bounce in to greet him sporting a 21st century version of a jogging suit and laying out some snappy patter like "Hey, hi (flutter, flutter), I'm Granny Judy! So what's coming down?"

It will indeed be miraculous if I say only "what's coming down" without gratuitously splicing it with a four-letter insertion. The jaded abuse of the once-forbidden corporal nouns and verbs has not been restricted to America's youth. As it is, my children have to put up with grannies whose vocabularies occasionally include words once considered the exclusive domain of sailors and truckdrivers.

Don't granddaughters deserve something more refined and sedate than that? How are we going to regale them with tales of our youth, if we are still trying to live it? How are we going to share with them the serenity that comes with maturing and accepting, if we are so willfully resisting the inevitable march of time?

Agile minds and fit bodies need not be indigenous to the young. But it would be a bit more tasteful if some of our senior agile minds did not feel they were best reflected by surgically lifted eyes, if we could disassociate the concept of mental agility from physical tautness. And if some of the post-50-year-old fit bodies did not bedeck themselves in thematic T-shirts and jeans in some desperate mimicry of their offspring's nubile offspring. It all seems just a trifle sad.

Which brings us back to the not-too-distant demise of that

genteel species, the blue-haired lady. There is just no one out there—not among today's grannies or us future grannies—who's going to let gray go to white and then reach for that bottle of blue.

We potential blue-bottlers will instead be frizzed and frosted and have our bifocals ground into our tinted contacts. We will wear bangle earrings under our hearing aids and we'll have jaunty painted toenails perched on the footrests of our rockers.

And when in fact we are obliged to depart the great here and now despite our heroic efforts to halt the unavoidable, those we will have left behind will surely bestow upon us that ultimate accolade: "Honestly, wasn't Granny ADORABLE for 97?"

2.

COPING WITH CONTEMPORARY REAL LIFE
(AND YOU THOUGHT IT GOT EASIER)

WHEN IT'S TOUGH TO FIGURE OUT
WHAT IS TRULY TASTEFUL

Buried in the furor of actress Robyn Douglass' recent suit against *Hustler* magazine was a wonderful nugget begging to be examined: the issue of Good Taste. Testimony pivotal to the proceedings came from witness David Sohn, a professor of English, who declared that much of the material in *Hustler* is in extremely bad taste. Sohn, of Evanston, was introduced as an Expert on Good Taste.

What a swell job. Wouldn't it be terrific to be a certifiable Expert on Good Taste? Obviously all of us think we are pillars of aesthetic sensibility: No one this side of the punkers sets out to embrace the offensive. Look around on any given day at Great America. That person in the lime shorts and puce plaid shirt actually finds that particular ensemble rather fetching.

This could lead one to believe that taste is relative, and yet this witness is brought in on the premise that there are immutable, objective standards of Good Taste.

Would that it were so. Good Taste is an extremely elusive commodity to nail down. I'm not even sure David Sohn (who has written 24 books and is very bright and genteel) has a handle on it. I conclude that because I called and asked this

Expert on Good Taste what *objets* he chose for his personal living environment.

The list began: a beige couch (artfully subtle); a Georgia O'Keeffe print (appropriate, but not pretentious); an Eames chair (an indisputable classic); an antique clock (so far, so good), and then . . . brown *shag* carpeting. Brown shag carpeting? Whither goes the credibility rating of an Expert on Good Taste who has brown shag carpeting?

This shag saga brings to mind the good-taste tale of Roberta. Her psychiatrist, Dr. Lewis, had an outstandingly ugly living room that his patients used as a waiting area. The ambience was distinctly '50s Hollywood Modern—bunches of blond wood free-form tables, sculpted foam chairs covered in cotton leopard prints, pole lamps galore—a festival of appalling aesthetics. Roberta wondered how she could turn her feelings over to a person with such nonstop bad taste in furnishings. What if he had equally bad taste in psyches? As she mulled this over, a curious fantasy began to take hold.

Surely Dr. Lewis was aware that this room assaulted his patients' sensibilities. Perhaps this excess of ugliness was merely a test of his patients' integrity. Clearly all Roberta had to do was screw up her courage and confront Dr. Lewis with the blatant truth: "Dr. Lewis, your living room is in the worst taste I've ever seen." And Dr. Lewis would look into her eyes and say with great calm, "Roberta, you're cured."

If only Good Taste were that clear-cut. But of course Dr. Lewis thought his living room was pretty spiffy, and David Sohn does not gag at the sight of brown shag carpeting. And I'm sure they would both walk into my house and say, "My God, did you see those mauve corduroy chairs?" Taste is a sliding-scale issue.

The Random House dictionary defines it as "a sense of what is fitting, harmonious, or beautiful; of what may be done or said without giving offense or committing an impropriety." But put three people in a room with a Grecian urn and an unclothed woman and you won't get any two to agree on what is harmonious, beautiful, or improper.

I wouldn't want my byline in *Hustler* for the same reason Robyn Douglass didn't want her photos there. But my version of terrible taste probably isn't shared by the million-plus *Hustler* readers. It would be wonderful if there were some shared standards, but as some philosopher-king said, "That's what makes the world go 'round, buddy."

Anyway, if everyone had my standards of taste, who'd marry all those guys at Great America wearing Bermudas with short dark socks?

WHEN BUYING A CAR PRESENTS YOU WITH MAJOR PHILOSOPHICAL INSIGHTS

I feel the same way about cars that I do about husbands. As soon as you stop being able to trust them, it's time to get rid of them. Granted, you'd rather have mistrust arise in the mechanical than the marital arena, but that doesn't lessen your sense of betrayal when a three-year-old car with a scant 20,000 miles on it starts wheezing and death-rattling and then dying on you. This infidelity is particularly painful when three years ago the betrayee waxed patriotic about supporting America's automotive industry, and the betrayer is one of Detroit's finest.

To add injury to insult, you find yourself in the distressing position of having to spend a gargantuan sum of money to replace something that gives you no aesthetic, sensory, or emotional gratification. An automobile is no more than a means of transport, and no less than mandatory if you happen to take your car-pool responsibilities seriously.

And though life is rife with noxious experiences, I'd have to say that ranking right up there with root-canal work and children's birthday parties is the ballet of B.S. you are forced to participate in when purchasing a new car.

Why isn't buying a car like buying a tie, or an eggplant, or a pair of pantyhose? You have a product, you have a price, and to obtain the product you pay the price—a simple, stress-free, decent exchange. But when buying a car, you leap instantly from the domain of decency into the domain of deceit. You have a product, you have a price, and to obtain the product you're *not* expected to pay the price. Instead you are expected to wade through a prescribed ritual of ignoble machinations guaranteeing that even the shiniest of new purchases will have an aura that is somewhat tarnished.

This time, however, instead of experiencing the usual sordid sensations of being poverty-stricken wallet-wise and integrity-wise, I actually emerged from the clutches of Sam the Salesman with a fabulously enriching life concept that I will present to you momentarily.

When I'm car shopping, I leave at home all jewelry, designer clothes, and accessories, and don my frowsiest duds. This ensures that Sam, who has more angles than an octagon, is duped into thinking I live with my husband in destitution, even though we are shopping for a brand-new car in 1983, when half the models cost a minimum of five figures.

We explain to Sam we're interested only in a bottom-of-the-line edition. Sam is highly sorry, but all he has on the lot is the souped-up glitz model that he happens to be able to *give* us for almost the same price—why don't you hop in and drive it? Slam.

I am suddenly behind the adjust-a-tilt wheel of a terrifyingly lush machine. I do not like lush machines with push-button digital pre-programmed everything, because as you increase your electronic electives you increase your Murphy's Law vulnerability. I especially do not like lush machines that talk. This car talks. It says, in the most patronizing female voice, things like "Your . . . gas . . . is . . .low" and "Your . . .

lights are . . . on." My husband sees no reason to pay money to have yet another patronizing female tell him he's screwed up.

Sam assures us the lady is an N/C (no charge) item. My husband asks Sam if the car is available without the lady. And that is when Sam comes up with the fabulously enriching life concept. Sam explains it's impossible to have the car without the lady; the lady is—are you ready for this—a *mandatory option.*

You need reflect only a moment to realize that a major philosophical nugget has been handed to you in an arid automobile showroom by a guy in an 80/20 polyester-cotton plaid. You've never had it presented with such clarity before, but what better definition of life itself than to see it as a series of *mandatory options?*

Of course, Sam's serene acceptance of the *mandatory option* philosophy of life was really only the 80/20 polyester-cotton way of saying "it's all karma." I just never knew there were any Buddhists selling cars.

IS IT POSSIBLE TO HAVE SHAVED LEGS AND PRINCIPLES TOO?

Even Gloria Steinem sometimes shaves her legs in winter. Winter surely offers us the optimum moment to pose the haunting philosophical inquiry: "Why am I shaving my legs?"

There are those who imply that a woman who opts for artificial sleekness is a sell-out. Fellow shavers, no longer is it necessary to search for some sense of justifiability when we defend the Sisyphean labors of leg shaving. I hope the following will provide some substantive responses to the most common charges leveled by the anti-shaving contingency.

Women shave just to please their men. This assumption is both facile and false. "I can't imagine not shaving," said Marie Q., a woman whose basic wardrobe is black cotton stockings and a full-length, six-piece nun's habit. Sister was incredulous that one would equate the absence of men in her life with the presence of fuzzy legs. In spite of the stereotypes, not all American men are totally inflexible on the to shave-or-not-to-shave issue. For instance, a man born and raised in the confines of Cleveland, Ohio, was smitten on a beach by a winsome Parisienne named Christine. Christine was a non-shaver. Christine was also topless. It's amazing what a great pair of breasts can do to break down the ostensible smooth-limb addiction of the average American male—even when he's from Cleveland.

Leg shaving is ridiculously time-consuming. A magazine editor tells the tale of taking along a woman photographer when he went to cover a story in a backwoods southern town. When they got to their sultry destination, the woman, who normally wore jeans in Chicago, put on a skirt and thereby unveiled an incredible pair of gorilla legs. The townsfolk did not take kindly to those legs. The townsfolk actually felt those legs were a blatantly hostile, big-city, nose-thumbing gesture by the photographer. And that evening when the locals got good and liquored up, they shared those sentiments with the photographer, requiring her to spend considerably more time and energy escaping their wrath than would have been required to have shaved her legs.

Leg shaving is futile. Lots of the best things in life are futile. Sexual gratification, for instance. We can have an evening crammed with orgiastic wonderment, and a couple days later we're lusting again. Culinary indulgence. Same story. Even a four-star meal does not stave off hunger for an indefinite period. Futility is hardly indigenous to the stubbly calf.

Women who shave are victims of a perverse sensibility about hair. No more than men are. Is there anyone more crazed, ashamed, and frantic than a man who is going bald? The woman who continues her regulation razoring in the dead of winter is not manifesting some insidious insecurity about her femaleness. She may be indulging in a bit of artifice, she may be perpetuating a somewhat arbitrary aesthetic, but she hardly qualifies as traitorous to the basic tenets of feminism.

Susan Brownmiller would disagree. This eloquent feminist author stopped shaving a few years ago, and yet is still unable to accept the unaesthetic results. "I look at my legs and know they are no longer attractive, not even to me," she says. But she stopped shaving "as a matter of principle."

What principle? The fact that hair grows on our legs does not make it physiologically or philosophically redeeming. Gunk grows on our teeth. Brushing it off does not exactly diminish our integrity.

Nor does shaving our legs in winter. We aren't doing it out of shame, or fear, or a sycophantic pandering to some male-imposed criterion. We're doing it only for ourselves. It happens to make us feel nice. This is not such a terrible thing.

Nobody ever said a bit of pampering isn't a worthy principle too. Not even Gloria Steinem.

WHEN THEY WANT YOU
TO TRADE IN YOUR BIKINIS
FOR BOXER SHORTS

Are you going to go for it? God, I hope not. Ladies, are you going to stand idly by and let an androgynous fashion designer destroy one of the last bastions of girly-girl apparel left in our business suit–sweat suit–crammed closets?

The ubiquitous Calvin Klein is waging out-and-out war on

. . . (blush) intimate apparel. From high atop his Manhattan atelier, Mr. K. has issued the edict: "Lingerie is a term of the past. [From now on] it's just underwear."

I hate to think of myself as "an old-fashioned girl," but as I go slogging into the '80s it becomes more and more apparent that this smarmy category does indeed suit me. I ignore all contemporary phobias and continue in my resolutely "old-fashioned" way to eat sugar, smoke the occasional cigarette, and tan my body. And though one day I may modernize and give up all or some of the above grievous weaknesses, I just can't see myself saying "so long" to silky, lovely underthings and opting for Calvin's locker room look in skivvies.

Have you seen the stuff? It's strictly for the pumping iron populace. Brightly colored cotton briefs highly reminiscent of cupless jockey shorts with the oh-so-sporty wide white elastic waistband stamped with the even more *sportif nom de* Calvin. Or should you be the type that leans toward transpiration (or transvestism), a pair of genuine mucho macho boxer shorts with a non-optional fly (guaranteed when worn to provoke an unavoidable attack of you-know-what envy).

And topping off these virilized bloomers is a plentiful array of jaunty, sleeveless . . . undershirts. Undershirts, I tell you. Listen, we may have burned our bras 15 years ago in a fit of firm-breasted feminist defiance, but now we are beyond 35, now we have borne children, now we (though less than bountifully endowed) are capitulating to the relentless pull of gravity, and now we are forced to acknowledge the truth: We do not even look close to our best in an undershirt. We require serious elastic. We require intricate crisscrosses. We require brassieres, Calvin, so why on earth are you giving us tank tops?

Why must the barbell look follow us into the boudoir too? Aren't we entitled to have this one final *Gone-with-the-Wind* layer of clothing in our lives? I never figured I'd share a sentiment with Marabelle Morgan or Phyllis Schlafly, but it causes me immense despair to think about all the upcoming heterosexual seductions in bedrooms strewn with the participants' virtually interchangeable underwear. Whither goes allure if our little indulgence in slink and come-hither is stomped on by designer versions of jockey shorts and deeze-'n'-doz-beer-guzzlers' undershirts?

Can we draw the line here? Can we say *no* to the inhabitants of fashion maven land who are insisting the onslaught of tough-broad bloomers will be the biggest thing to hit the lingerie (pardon my anachronism) department since pantyhose rendered girdles and garter belts defunct? Are we going to support a look that gives us no support? Are we going to succumb to a style that is dubious even on the finest of *Flashdance* figures? For god's sake, ladies, we've got his tie, we've got his briefcase, we've got his man-in-the-gray-flannel-suit in four or five uninteresting colors, so do you think we could possibly stay out of his drawers (pun flagrantly intended)?

Next thing you know we'll be wearing some Seventh Avenue wacko's version of cordovan wing tips.

And then if there's any justice among the undergarment gods, the ads will probably be reading: The Maidenform *Man*—You Never Know Where He'll Turn Up."

WHEN YOU ALMOST SELL OUT
FOR STATUS

It's always these murky, mini-moral dilemmas that nail you—the Lost and Found dilemmas of life. You know, the dilemma you're in when your kid has lost a week-old pair of size 3 Nike tennis shoes with red trim—and what do you find in the Lost and Found but a week-old pair of size 3 Nike tennis shoes with blue trim? And you can't help but (1) linger, (2) ponder, and what you do on (3) determines how you emerge from this murky mini-moral dilemma—pristine or corrupted.

Admittedly, no one's scorecard is 100 in the pristine department, but recently I just missed racking up mucho points in the corruption column. I met a woman wearing a watch I had coveted for years—a smashing Piaget stainless and gold number so chic and so costly that I'd only seen it in the pages of glossy periodicals, but never on a real, live arm.

Yesterday it was on a real, live arm, and being a model of well-mannered discretion, I lurched over to the owner of the arm and screeched, "My God! I love that watch. It's been my fantasy for ages!"

"Thanks," said the soignée blond. And then she paused, leaned forward conspiratorially, and whispered, "It's a fake. It cost $75 at this little place downtown."

Myriad emotions coursed through me. Euphoria: Surely I could scrape $75 together and get the watch of my dreams. Loathing: Was I a big enough jerk to knowingly pay that kind of money for a guaranteed fake? Confusion: What did I lust after—the Piaget's exterior design, its interior quality, or its implied status?

When you are raised, as I was raised, in the down-home Hills of Beverly, California, where even the household help carried Vuitton, you either continue to clutter your life with meaningful insignias and initials on clothes and cars and clutch bags or you say *ciao* to all that and go resolutely generic. I've been wearing the same generic gold watch since the Class of '65 got its diplomas.

It is not a watch that turns heads or raises eyebrows. It does not tell you that I am a classy lady. It tells you only the time. And though I have succumbed to ownership of two Polo T-shirts (at $6 apiece in Hong Kong, who could resist?), because of my sturdy, no-name timepiece, I've managed to hold on to a shred of moral superiority over addictive status seekers. (One gets one's moral superiority where one can.)

Designer anything, from jeans to towels to chocolates, ostensibly indicates elegance, but most of this is mass-produced chic and can be purchased for a two-figure price tag. Every self-respecting mall-teen has had someone's name stitched across his denimed tush or had some reptile or stitched-on steed gallop across his chest. Thirty bucks and panache (of a sort) are theirs.

But if you discount the Mercedes and Jaguars and stick to the wearables, the serious status items that, due to their hefty price tag, separate the men from the mall-teens are those quasi-canonized chronometers by Rolex, Cartier, and the aforementioned Piaget. And considering that your basic $35 year-guaranteed Timex can do the same job, one could buy a new Timex annually for 30 years for the same price as any of these baubles for bluebloods-in-training. But one would not have the desired hauteur of a Piaget-ed person. And if the truth be known, it was hauteur I was hoping to buy for $75.

Hauteur, however, does not fit in my life. Imagine walking into a newspaper office, surrounded by fellow underpaid journalists, wearing a watch supposedly costing at least a month's salary. One look and they'd think (1) I had a very warped set of monetary priorities or (2) it was a fake and I had an even more warped set of moral priorities.

And so, as I once refused the temptation of the blue-trimmed Nikes, I have refused the temptation of the counterfeit Piaget. But don't ask whether I did it because of impeccable ethics or because I just couldn't bear selling out my self-righteousness for 75 bucks.

CONFESSIONS OF A SECOND CITY CITIZEN

Sitting in a Third Avenue movie house years ago, I remember laughing smugly while New York City made cinematic fools out of Sandy Dennis and Jack Lemmon in *The Out of Towners.* I had put in my time on the IRT, was familiar with the idiosyncratic hours and pathways of hazard in Central Park, and had even nabbed a rent-controlled apartment 12 hours before it was listed in the *Village Voice.* My urban savvy quotient was at a lifetime high.

But last week, after 14 years as a non–New York resident, I discovered that the moves and attitudes needed for mastery of Manhattan atrophy with disuse and you are back to square one, a total hayseed. This is not the way you expect to feel when six of the intervening years were spent in major European capitals and the remaining eight in the dynamic, albeit second, city of Chicago. But three days in New York made me feel as if I had just gotten off the bus from Ashtabula.

First of all, you lose the rhythm. That crazed, frenetic gait that makes "brisk" look like a slow-motion word. Anywhere else it might be considered neurotically frantic, but in New York it's simply the regulation pace to keep from being trampled.

One night I was meeting a California friend who had never been east of Palm Springs. Knowing the trauma an L.A. freeway person would have coping with public transportation, I volunteered to escort him on his maiden subway voyage. With some condescension, I explained the intricacies of express and local service and crosstown shuttles. I may have been great on routes, but apparently I was real rusty on reflexes.

It's still a bit hazy, but as I recall, the train screeched in, hordes spewed out, hordes surged in, and zap—the train was gone. Over. And two dazed rubes from America's second- and third-largest metropolises remained on the platform. Duke Ellington notwithstanding, you cannot always take the A train.

Second, you lose the determination and fortitude that enable Manhattanites to overcome enormous logistical obstacles to have something most of the rest of us have by simply waking up on Saturday morning: a good weekend. The stamina required to make multiple-transport journeys from city to slopes or city to shore in order to "get out of the city" is nearly as herculean as the mental acrobatics they must go through to convince themselves that the entire dehumanizing exodus is worth it.

One could comprehend if the destinations, once reached, resonated with serenity. But they are cramped and crowded with people celebrating their escape from the cramped and crowded city. Chicago's beaches or Wisconsin's slopes aren't necessarily less densely populated, but enjoying them doesn't usually require torturous journeys or half-shares in houses with people you despise by season's end.

And though our shores and slopes aren't exempt from urban wackos, Big Apple nutsiness remains the unchallenged titleholder (for cities east of Las Vegas).

Understand, this is no chastisement, but merely the observations of a Second City citizen who fancied herself rather cosmopolitan until this return visit to New York. Painful as it was to admit that I was embarrassingly out of sync with the city, I assumed my secret would be safe. Wrong-o.

Following a meeting with one of the more respected magazines in town, I sashayed out into the street feeling drenched in professionalism and big-city smarts. I was a vision in silk and suede, and my attaché case contained that morning's edition of the *Times*. I swooped into a cab and, in tones leaning offensively toward regal, said, "Take me to 68th and Lex."

The cabbie turned around, gave me a perfunctory once-over, let out a sigh reeking of patronization, and inquired, "So, lady. Where ya in from?"

Note: the entire proceeds from this column were donated involuntarily to a masterful pickpocket in Bloomingdale's. A rube by any other name is still a. . . .

RESISTING THE LURE OF HYPOCHONDRIAC HEAVEN

※

It's hard enough to get through the morning ablutions without this, too. The workout, the shower, the teeth, the vitamins, and now . . . *ta dumm* . . . the blood pressure.

Have you seen the ads? We are now being enouraged to check our blood pressure on a daily basis before heading out the door. Timex, the company that kept John Cameron Swayze employed for years scooping watches from fish bowls and gave us the $99 computer, is again in the vanguard of consumer gizmo-dom.

For $59.95, you can be the proud owner of a home blood pressure monitor, because, as the ads say, "When those numbers look great, you feel great."

Now let's be candid. There are only four numbers in the world with enough emotional clout to make us feel great or nongreat: our weight, our age, our income, and the number of people we've slept with. And we lie about them all. But how many of us are concerned with, or want to be concerned with, our blood pressure? Blood pressure is what they do to you at the gynecologist before they get to the embarrassing part. Blood pressure is what great-grandmothers talk about after they've discussed whether the prune juice worked. Blood pressure is bad when it's high and bad when it's low; and the less I know about it, the better.

Suppose you're having one of those February days when your perspective on life is pewter, and the bed is looking awfully tempting. You aren't running a fever, you've no precise pains, but hark! Your handy-dandy home blood pressure monitor awaits. Pump . . . pump . . . pump . . . ahhhhh. Your reading: 150 over 90. Ten degrees above normal. You dive into the bed; after all, you're practically terminal. I tell you, this product takes us two giant steps forward into hypochondriac heaven.

Now, in my heart of hearts (found with my home stethoscope), I know this blood pressure monitor has been brought to us for loftier purposes than abetting office absenteeism. It's simply the latest product from the $2.5 billion home health care industry.

Because two million visits to doctors each year are a waste of time and therefore a waste of money, the home health care industry has been born to encourage people to use their own resources for dealing with common ailments and thus free up doctors for serious stuff.

But, hard-core hypochondriacs will always be there; this just gives them lots of gear to monitor their maladies. And while it may temporarily deter them from clogging the waiting rooms, I imagine it's just a matter of time until they're again ringing up the pros.

Only now, instead of their whiny, vague complaints, they'll be able to go in for specific, digitally confirmed lamentations. But it's to us borderline hypochondriacs that this high-tech home health hardware poses the most insidious menace. With no means to substantiate our minor aches and pains, most of us ignore them, and at least we manage to remain functional.

It used to be enough to be funtional, but with this free-floating fitness fascination of recent years, chugging along with a few normal imperfections (bleeding gums, corrugated thighs, hyperventilation after a sprint around the block) just won't do. Now most of us are overly depressed, overly impressed, or overly obsessed with our bodies. And I do worry that we borderline types are destined to become full-tilt fitness fetishists as the speculums and otoscopes pile up in our little black bags at home.

I don't know. In my day, playing doctor was a lot more fun.

MAKING PEACE WITH PROGRESS

It was hard not to feel slightly victimized. Last month I read of the demise of two of my favorite things.

First, the Yellow Pages. Some people relax with a crossword puzzle, some with a sitcom, some with a six-pack. I may be warpy, but I relax with the Yellow Pages. It is a comprehensive way to consider options—do you want Chinese or Italian tonight?—a leisurely way to get the lay of the land, and a split-second way to help you out of a non-911 disaster. But now some cities are beginning to use call-services that rely on computerized business directories and it's only a matter of time 'til the Yellow Pages goes the way of the blue whale.

Item No. 2 on the list of endangered species is the manual typewriter. Smith-Corona has stopped producing them. I spend more time each day with my manual than with my man. And while I've always known Thomas was irreplaceable, I never thought my manual would be.

An admitted curmudgeon about technological advancement, I'm just one of those types who needs a little time to meander into the world of Progress.

But with imminent demise looming over two items vital to my quality of life, it became clear that my meandering days were over. My hand was being forced, and I was going to have to leap into the electronic breach and embrace Progress.

So, mustering my courage and my credit card, I did it. I bought a videocassette recorder. I was one of the 6 percent— in the vanguard at last—of American television viewers who were "going video."

The last time "video" was in my life was in 1952. Every day after school my best friend and I would ritualistically reenact our marriage vows with the captain we loved. In 1952, Video was my last name.

After that, unless the picture tube on the TV blew, video

was a pretty peripheral concept in lifestyle. Now video *is* a life-style. I know, because as soon as I brought that VCR into the house, it began to control my life.

For starters, no one but our digital-minded 12-year-old could follow the operating instructions. For hundreds of dollars, I had the privilege of being at a pre-teen's mechanical mercy.

For those same hundreds, I also had the pleasure of stepping into an entirely new arena for family dissension. Hardly a night passed when the *Dumbo* segment of the family wasn't at cinematic odds with the "Fame" segment. Hardly a morning went by when the "Fame" segment wasn't wailing about being denied carte blanche to tape the "All My Children" shows she was missing while attending algebra.

Hardly a Saturday night went by when the master of the house wasn't proposing to bring in gamey X-rated entertainment. Hardly a Sunday went by when master and mistress weren't grudgingly at odds over whose turn it was to run the cassettes back to the video library.

Is this Progress? No wonder I'd resisted it for so long. It was a veritable Pandora's box.

Note that I said "was," because I hit a technological turning point. I decided to master this machine that had been pushing my buttons all month. I finally understood. Progress isn't possession of the gadget. It's subjugation of it.

You should see me now. I can cut through commercials with the speed of an Olympic sprinter and throw "Love Boat" into reverse with the defiance of a Roman cab driver. There's something positively exhilarating about breakfasting with Carson or dining with Donahue. No wonder they call it Me-TV. What a rush to finally bend TV to my schedule.

I can barely contain my excitement. Every night I whisper conspiratorially to my husband, "Hey, honey, do you want to come upstairs and . . . time-shift with me?"

That's the great thing about being such a recent convert to Progress. I can't take it for granted. It still feels *so* sinful.

3.

GRIST
FOR THE
MARRIAGE
MILL

MONEY: THE ULTIMATE
DOMESTIC DETONATOR

·Ⅰ·

The weekend has begun. It's Friday night, you and your spouse are in front of the fire, sipping on a soothing something with enough alcoholic content to assuage the cumulative anxieties of a week in the office, and guess what happens? Despite the vino, despite the flaming hearth, despite your mutual need for some conjugal comfort, dissension rears its grizzly head. The ever-provocative topic of *money* has come up.

"Listen," says your stressed-out significant other, "do we have to talk about money now? All it's going to do is ruin the weekend. And I could really use a good weekend." (So who couldn't use a really good weekend?) "Let's discuss this some other time."

Like when? There is no moment that has an all's-right-with-the-world ambience lasting long enough to withstand the guaranteed explosions the topic of finances always kicks off. You could have just completed the most innovative, acrobatically convoluted sexual favor for someone and if the post-passion murmuring wends its way toward wampum, watch out. All the points you may have just scored for wonder-

59

fulness will be zapped. Or you could have just received a non-occasion flower bouquet, but when the Visa bill is spotted on your desk, connubial bliss is smashed to smithereens. Money is the ultimate domestic detonator.

There are several reasons for this. The main one, of course, is that money is not just money. It represents a lot more serious stuff than purchasing power. Serious stuff like control, commitment, and trust. Not to mention your Basic World View.

Basic World View generally boils down to the old is-the-glass-half-empty-or-half-full proposition. Suppose you've just gotten an unexpected $1,000 Christmas bonus and the idea of a week in Ixtapa, Mexico, strikes you as a reasonable way of disposing of said $1,000. Who could argue with that? Only the person you were planning to take along. Because that person is adamant that $1,000 should go directly into the maybe-someday-I'll-need-this-for-a-nursing-home fund. You already have a respectable amount in the someday fund, and you were sort of counting on doing some today spending. No such luck.

According to your disaster-is-just-around-the-corner spouse, there will never be enough. You pour more in, and this person just gets a bigger glass—that way it's always half-empty and the despair quotient remains stable.

Then there's control. Even the most non-Machiavellian person in the world gets a major jolt being the financial potentate in a marriage. Usually the partner who gets first crack at pulling the purse strings is the partner bringing in the biggest chunk of income. After being beaten on all week by corporate creeps, is it not exhilarating to demand some accountability from someone? What do you mean $90 for electricity? This implies the potentate could have kept the joint well lit for about $14.50 and this affords the non-potentate a splendid opportunity to launch into high defensiveness as if she or he had frittered away the last dime on baubles and caviar.

And then there's commitment. Show me a marriage where

the money isn't pooled and I'll show you only a meaningful relationship, not a real marriage. Once the intensity and the romance go and you settle down to it, one of the most significant ties that bind is the financial one. Ask Joanna Carson. Couples who won't couple their resources barely even test their capacity to trust. There's sex, and there's in-laws, and there's child-raising, but more than almost anything, it's the business of marriage that makes marriage such a tricky business.

Which is why there's only one answer to the haunting question "When is the optimum moment to talk about money like a rational grown-up?"

Never is when, darling. Never.

❊

RESIGNING FROM SUPPORTIVE CARROT PEELING

❊

Dieting is very bad for a marriage. It is especially bad when only one person in the marriage is on the diet. Obviously, the rigors of culinary abstinence are horrific for the dieter, but no one ever considers the plight of the nondieting spouse. We aren't necessarily among those hateful, naturally thin people. Often we are people who exercise a lot, or sometimes we are people who are perfectly happy to be a bit plump. The point is that we don't happen to be on a diet.

And dieting spouses tend to grow hostile about this. Frequently they try to make us feel guilty. This always works. And because we love our dieting spouses and want svelteness to be theirs, we clear the shelves of Frango mints, Häagen-Dazs, potato chips, and pastrami. After all, what's a little deprivation when it comes to love?

Thus, in the name of love, we nondieters plunge into the diet-support syndrome. We clean celery and peel carrots with a vengeance. We cook the most boring meals on record or spend hours concocting, gram by gram, some pseudo-sauce from Scarsdale. We spend fortunes on fresh fish and lean cuts of meat and perform highly distasteful chores, such as trimming the skin and fat from poultry.

We even start drinking alone, because the caloric consequences prohibit a shared cocktail hour. And try as we might—with candles, Perrier in wine glasses, six green beans artfully crisscrossed with a rosy sliver of pimiento, all nestled next to a slice of grilled something—we can't fool those loved ones on a diet. They're hungry . . . and grumpy. And when they diet, there's hell to pay. Doors slam, voices raise, and we all tiptoe around them on those awful mornings when the scales haven't acquiesced to their pound-a-day program.

By the time their goal is realized, the rest of the family also is feeling emotionally emaciated. Don't think we haven't suffered, too. That is why, dear dieters, we feel outraged and betrayed when you abandon your hard-earned trimness and begin to slowly nudge the scales upward again.

How do you think we feel to awaken at two in the morning to the aroma of Polish sausage sizzling away? All we can think of is our hands, chapped and ruddy from peeling pounds of carrots. All we can think of is that fishing rod or sweater we never bought because we had spent so much on chopped sirloin during the month of dietude.

In a society rife with support groups and networks, to whom do we, the loved ones of dieters, turn? From whom do we gain the moral fiber to hand over the carrot peeler and say, "Honey, I love you, but do it yourself. It's your diet this time"?

From whom do we gain the emotional fortitude to say, "I'm with you 100 percent, but it has been 14 days and the kids and I are going out for a carbohydrate fix tonight"? From whom do we gain the serenity not to be riddled by disappointment when the bacon is cooking at midnight and, to add insult to injury, the congealed grease on the griddle is there the next morning?

To all you beloved dieters out there, I plead with you: Give us a break. Our nondieting hasn't made us smug, but we can't continue to feel guilty about it either. Jack Sprat and his wife worked out an equitable arrangement with a minimum of psychological abuse.

Maybe we can, too.

REVEALED: THE REAL SECRET BEHIND SECRET KEEPING

I love two people very much. One is my friend and one is my husband. And for a year, I kept my friend's love life secret from my husband. And it was hard, and confusing, and I'm very glad it's over.

Last month my friend herself told my husband what I'd been keeping secret. He wasn't even terribly surprised. What surprised him and perplexed him and wounded him was that I could have kept a secret from him. He could NEVER, he said, keep one from me. I defended my secret-keeping with the usual confidentiality/loyalty rationale, but he didn't buy it 100 percent. Maybe he is right. Maybe we need all that lofty reasoning because secrets make us feel so conflicted.

Secrets have always had bad press. From pigtail and pinafore days to tell-it-like-it-is times, secrecy has had slimy and cowardly connotations, be it mean-spirited gossip or world-altering conspiracies. We teach our children secrets aren't nice because they impose exclusion and because most kids' secrets tend to be rooted in a budding bitchiness.

Obviously, certain secrets have always been socially acceptable: surprise parties, Santa Claus, the first trimester of pregnacy. Those are nonnefarious enough and are all ultimately revealed at the right time. My friend's secret too had a right time for revelation, but *she* had to determine that. My role was to walk the ethical tightwire between forsaking a confidentiality and lying by omission.

Ethical tightwires constantly crisscross our private and professional lives and are always tricky to negotiate. Certain professions—doctors, lawyers, men of the cloth—have fairly clear-cut codes of confidentiality. But even for them it gets murky. Terminal illness strikes, and doctors must decide which patient or family to tell, which patient or family to protect. Protection is always the great rationale, but there's a mighty fine line between protecting a secret and perpetrating a disservice. The old do-I-tell-my-best-friend-her-husband-was-out-with-someone-else dilemma.

It happened to my friend Stanley, an advertising agency vice president. He was called for a reference on an accountant whom he had once employed. The accountant did not leave Stanley's agency under the most kosher circumstances. He had been caught embezzling, was convicted, and served his time. Whom to protect? The accountant who was simply trying to start his life again, or the potential employer, who was at least entitled to know that this man had broken the law and had paid his dues. Wouldn't Stanley have felt entitled to the same information? He chose to protect the accountant's secret. By choosing that, did he betray the potential employer?

By protecting my friend's secret, was I betraying my marriage? Certainly, *not* knowing her secret wasn't harmful to my husband. But by guarding my intimacy with her, did I diminish my intimacy with him? I don't know. How do you maintain the delicate balance between fidelity to friend and fidelity to spouse? Do you decide on the basis of which relationship you honor most? Impossible. It's apples and oranges. Is living with unspoken truths the same as living with lies? Oh God, it gets very confusing and abstract and philosophical.

I wanted to believe that I guarded my friend's secret for noble ethical concepts like honor, and loyalty, and discretion. But it's beginning to dawn on me that it may have had less to do with ethics than with ego. There's something very seductive about being chosen as an audience of one for soul baring. And perhaps there was something not only unnoble, but downright Machiavellian about keeping her secret from my husband.

Suppose he responded judgmentally and decided (1) my friend was a rotten human being and (2) if she was rotten, maybe I was less than worthy, too. All that ethical philosophizing and I finally had to ask myself just whom and what I was protecting: my friend's confidentiality, my husband's innocence, or maybe my own backside. Within every philosopher king there's a subliminal streak of pragmatism.

⁂

SAYING "SO LONG" TO THE CHERRY AMES STUDENT NURSE SCHOOL OF LOVING

⁂

"And this time, I'm not signing up to be the guy's nurse," said my pal—not defiantly, but with calm, cool certitude. And we both knew what a resounding breakthrough moment it was. She finally said "no thank you" to one of the all-time corrosive delusions that somehow remains operative for a majority of otherwise intelligent females. Namely, that when you love someone, his pain becomes your pain, and you can make a whole lot of that pain go away when you love him hard enough and true enough.

It's a country-western frame of mind, except that it even transcends the "Stand by Your Man" school of loving and leaps into the neurotic assumption that you are the guy's guardian angel/lifesaver. It's a highly tempting role. And highly self-indulgent. And highly self-destructive.

Tempting because all of us fancy the concept of saving the bird with the broken wing. Lurking in even the most petulant, princessy among us is a Mother Teresa just waiting to leap out. Just-divorced men frequently bring out the Mother Teresa in many women. Misunderstood married men tend to bring out the Mother Teresa in younger women. And shy, inarticulate, repressed, highly screwed-up men have always brought out the Mother Teresa in every woman. Every woman has at least one great nursing stint in her. I mean, how many chances do we get to feel downright beatific? There are few roles quite as seductive as chief saviorette.

And few roles as self-indulgent. Where do we get the audacity to assume that we are so swell, so special, and so omnipotent that we alone have been put on this earth to put Humpty Dumpty back together again? That does take an incredible capacity for arrogance.

And an incredible capacity for self-sabotage. Because as anyone who has ever put in her time as somebody's psychological punching bag in the great campaign to Establish His Self-Esteem knows, you never come out unscathed. Sometimes you never even come out. Or you finally realize that playing nurse has only one consistent result. You usually end up feeling about as anguished as the patient. And you usually end up feeling real ticked off. At him for being the same old lunkhead, and at yourself for being lunkhead enough to put up with the original lunkhead.

So you have two choices. You can stay permanently ticked off and the next time you meet a man who is needy you can do your best Joan Rivers imitation and tell him to just grow up. Or (and here comes the hard part) you can figure out the difference between being supportive and being an obsessive caretaker. This is not easy. This is not easy because at some level we women have a very hard time putting the men in charge of their own depression or their own dilemmas or their own development. For instance: *The Peter Pan Syndrome*, a recent book describing the phenomenon of men who resist growing up, was addressed not to those men who remain residents of Never-Never Land, but to the women who are coping with those 30-year-old adolescents. This entire book was rooted in the sad-but-true premise that most women appoint themselves liable for the emotional equilibrium of the adult male person in their lives.

Until they reach the point my pal did. When void of rancor, void of resentment, and void of unrealistic resolutions, she said "so long" to a lifetime of nursing. So far it's working well. She no longer is clucking over and ministering to the guy, and that's finally allowing him to do what the doctors always have advised.

Heal thyself, sir, heal thyself.

※

TO GIVE—OR NOT TO GIVE—AN X-RATED BIRTHDAY PRESENT

※

He's having one of those big birthdays, the kind with a zero at the end. And the last thing in the world he wants is some major commemorative gala. This is a man who truly likes but a handful of people, and who would be appalled by anything resembling a public acknowledgement that statistically he's about to step into a new chronological time zone.

Your options for occasion observation are definitely restricted to the private domain. A romantic dinner at an overpriced restaurant? Not too creative. A new watch? He hates jewelry. A week's vacation? He travels for work. What you want is something intimate, innovative, and in town.

You decide to take him 15 minutes away from your Father-Knows-Best street to the Sybaris Inn—a "love" motel where even people with the poshest demographic qualifications succumb to the unique blend of the kinky and the deluxe. You've heard the "adult" ambience there ensures that everyone rises (sorry) to the occasion.

For a mere sliver of what it costs to hire a room, pay a band, and offer refreshment to 50 boorish party guests, you and the birthday boy, clad in your respective birthday suits, partake of the following: a 22-foot swimming pool in your room; a connecting whirlpool with enough strategically placed jets to make you understand why Esther Williams never got out of the water; an endlessly undulating king-size water bed; mirrors on ceiling and walls; a steam room; and a closed-circuit TV channel featuring 24 hours of decidedly nonsoft porn.

Lest your nose be wrinkled in disgust over this last option, remember it is an option, and that in spite of your inherent resistance to most things X-rated, this place is definitely not tacky. It's just completely private and completely effective in combatting almost any modern-day malaise—from birthday blues to the garden-variety erosion of the old romantic/erotic edge.

You remember the old romantic/erotic edge, don't you? It's the first one that crumbled as your relationship segued into the yawny comforts of compatibility and persistent demands of parenthood. Passion can get awfully past tense when you've got resident offspring.

The place is terrific. On a scale of 1 to 10, it's 100. Note: neither you nor the birthday boy is a chronic sensualist. "Afterglow" for you usually consists of a ham and cheese sandwich and a restorative bottle of Coke. So both of you are a bit surprised at all the repressed ribaldry still lurking in these not-too-taut bodies.

While watching the X-rated film, you can't help but roar over the awesome attributes of some of the stars and some of the amazing incongruities Mother Nature offers between neck-up appearances and navel-down realities. However, after an hour of this visual fare when nary a prurient interest is left unfilmed, it becomes evident that doing it is a lot more fun than viewing it.

And the birthday boy is really into it. You're like two horny adolescents with no curfew just turned loose in a Disneyland of debauchery. This man whose most athletic activity during any given week is filling in the crossword puzzle emerges a born-again voluptuary. The guest of honor thinks he has died and gone to heaven.

What greater gift can you give your mid-life man than a chance to dispute the statistics that he's several years on the down side of his peak? Tonight anyway, he's clearly back up on the old sexual summit.

Happy birthday, honey.

THE REAL TRAGEDY BEHIND THREE DYING CHAMELEONS

Little Ralphie and his daddy have three pet chameleons. The chameleon food is all gone. Ralphie's daddy works full time. Ralphie's mommy works full time. But the chameleons are starving. So guess who drives to the store to get the worms to feed the chameleons that belong to Ralphie and Daddy. Not Ralphie and not Daddy.

Screech! Mommy hits the brakes and heads home. She is furious. Not with Ralphie and not with Daddy. With herself. Her consciousness ostensibly was raised ten years ago, but what became clear in this chameleon chronicle was that apparently her unconsciousness has remained mired in the fossilized assumption that though Daddy may do the dishes, the bottom-line responsibility for the homestead and the well-being of all its creatures great and small—kids to chameleons—was still hers.

Gentlemen, don't panic. Phase 2 (or is it 12?) of The Movement is here and, for want of a catchier label, is called "unconsciousness raising." But instead of steeling yourselves against another onslaught of stridency, perhaps you can assist in dismantling some of the archaic axioms under which men and women are still operating.

After all, it's the 1980s and one would assume antediluvian preconceptions of "men's work" and "women's work" would have bitten the dust. But consider the following statistics from a recent Merit Report of two-career households:

- When asked who should take out the garbage, a resounding 52 percent said the husband, 4 percent said the wife, and 42 percent said it should be shared.
- When asked who should stay home with a sick child, 1 percent said the husband, an appalling 62 percent said the wife, and 34 percent said it should be shared.
- When asked who should prepare the meals, 1 percent said the husband, 46 percent said the wife, and 51 percent said it should be shared.
- When asked who *does* prepare the meals, 2 percent said the husband, a scandalous 72 percent said the wife, and 26 percent said it was shared.

Adorable. What we have here is some numbing numerical confirmation that none of us has come a long way, baby. If we had, how could 52 percent of us think taking out garbage is men's work? Most women have hauled heavier and handled sloppier items than garbage. Garbage and meal-making and temperature-taking are highly androgynous activities. And yet in the case of two full-time Evanston pediatricians married to each other, why does the mommy pediatrician always stay home with ill offspring?

And in the case of the "liberated" lady lawyer who leaves a

note that says "home late—potatoes in microwave, steak in fridge," who made sure there was dinner? Daddy may have done the marketing last weekend, but who wrote the list? Daddy may have picked up Ralphie from the sitter, but who made the arrangements?

What is shamefully odd is that even women younger than 35, who supposedly subscribed to all the Steinemesque statutes, subliminally adhere to some Paleozoic principle that puts the onus of organizational chieftainship on them.

To varying degrees we all can acknowledge that Daddy has become an active participator, but when is he going to become an active orchestrator?

Not until we *let* him. Because it isn't simply that he refuses to assume any accountability; it's that somehow we still aren't able to give up accountability. It may be guilt about abandoning the old script, but given the perverse sense of power and control in being chief planner, it may be just a touch Machiavellian, too. Think about it.

That's what unconsciousness-raising is all about. And it will take getting rid of a lot more than three dead chameleons to get it raised.

PARDON ME, BUT COULD YOU AMPUTATE MY DUSTCLOTH?

It's not easy being compulsively neat, you know. It means a constant, futile, and depressing battle to keep things "just so." It means a constant, futile, and depressing choice between being the silently suffering martyr who resentfully picks up after your less-than-orderly co-residents and being the hateful shrew who unceasingly harangues them. No one likes a compulsively neat person—not even another compulsively neat person.

That is why they always live with, marry, and parent chronic slobs. It's one of those predictable, mundane yin/yangs of real life. I would even venture that a significant percentage of divorces occurs when two slobs or two compulsives erroneously hook up. Two compulsives, with no one to scream at, are deprived of their intrinsic need to sanctimoniously straighten up after a sloppy spouse. Denied their regulation dose of self-righteousness, they seem to lose their *raison d'être*. Two slobs, with no one to yell at them, admittedly can revel in their refuse for days on end but ultimately are forced to do their own cleaning, an endeavor that goes distinctly against their squalor-tolerant souls. In both instances, the basic nature of slob and compulsive alike is negated if they attempt to escape their Odd Couple destiny.

It is destiny, you know. Hard-core compulsives always are drawn to people who are incredibly cavalier about the Order of Things. For instance, the woman I have chosen as my absolute best friend in the world actually is capable of leaving a carful of groceries melting outside while she grabs a beer and settles in for a 20-minute phone chat. In my wildest, warpiest, most caution-to-the-wind daydreams, I could never pull that off. It's such an extravagant defiance of good housekeeping. It's so breathtakingly insouciant. It's so unfathomably appalling. It's so truly admirable.

Yes, admirable. Because in our heart of meticulous hearts, there probably isn't a fanatically fastidious person who wouldn't love to say "so long" to sponges and scrupulousness and simply learn to wallow. *Wallow* is on permanent sabbatical from our emotional vocabulary. We gaze in absolute wonder upon those who can read *The New Yorker* amid a sea of scummy day-old dishes, brimming ashtrays, jaundiced periodicals, and gritty laundry. And while, publicly, we look with disdain upon these litter lovers, we secretly covet their ability to maintain serenity in such slovenly surroundings. Clearly they are the great well-adjusted—if God had wanted the world to be tidy, would he have invented the Sunday paper?—and we are the truly crazed.

Messy people can accept the inherent chaos of the cosmos and long ago have given up trying to control it. Their world view is firmly rooted in the McDonald's Philosophy of Life: they deserve a break today. Compulsive cleaner-uppers, on the other hand, never feel deserving of a respite—not until the laundry is folded, the groceries are put away, the dishes are done, the kiddies are tucked in, and on and on. Oh, we may nurture the fantasy of breaking out and doing something rash, such as leaving the bed unmade all weekend, but for 86 percent of us, it is viscerally impossible to execute.

No, our lot is not an easy one. We don't like being chronic curmudgeons. We are fully aware that we could have become fluent in Japanese in the same number of hours we have devoted to nagging our rumpled loved ones. And yet we can't stop ourselves. Why haven't they organized a Neataholics Anonymous?

Slobs are viewed by the world with great benevolence and affection, but no one ever refers to one of us as "that lovable old compulsive." I guess you can't blame them. Who could love a woman addicted to squeezing the toothpaste from the bottom? Only a guy addicted to squeezing from the middle.

DULL IS ALL THE EXCITEMENT YOU CAN TAKE

Last month the Ten Dullest Americans list came out. What a thrill to know that being boring is now considered award-worthy. I have always had a predilection for the brown-shoes people in life. No doubt that is some sort of backlash to having spent my formative years in the high glitz of Los Angeles, where mothers wore cleavages to PTA meetings and never had the same last names as their kids. When you grow up in a place like that, it's only inevitable that you'll be passionate about sturdy, no-frills fellows—the VW guys of the world.

You know what I mean. These are the guys who still don't eat sushi, have never jogged, worn a pink Polo, or been to a Club Med. They have no aspirations for a Rolex and their idea of a great honeymoon is three days in Niagara Falls. These guys have never used *impact* as a verb, never been to a shrink, wouldn't touch a light beer, and always buy the same pair of wing-tip cordovans.

These are solid people. These are men who do not own or operate blow dryers, still haven't used up the bottle of Old Spice they bought for the senior prom, and wouldn't think of leaving their shirt front unbuttoned to artfully display a hirsute chest. They do not panic when they pass a mirror to pat their remaining 47 strands of you're-not-fooling-anyone hair into place over their bald spot. They can live with bald. And anyway, these guys don't need mirrors because they are always in blue oxford-cloth shirts with tan corduroys. Dull men may lack sartorial chic, but no one will ever taunt them with photos from their sideburn-and-Nehru-jacket days.

They know that flash has a built-in sudden mortality rate. They know for sure that if they raced out to buy the last word in fashion or foodstuffs, by the time they got it home it already would be the second-to-last-word. Dull men not only don't eat quiche, they still aren't really sure what it is. They eat meat (well-done), potatoes, iceberg lettuce salad, and orange gelatin with mini-marshmallows for dessert. Not a *nouvelle* morsel on their menu, not a Cuisinart on the counter. Dull men never argue the merits of Hunan vs. Sichuan—they consider a takeout order of egg foo yung to be a peak ethnic dining experience. God bless 'em.

Admittedly, dull men are awfully placid. But this actually is a great point in their favor, as they tend to be exempt from fashionable neuroses that haunt the chronically trendy. Dull men, for example, do not feel threatened or inadequate in bed because they never read any of those sex manuals that talk about "pleasuring" a partner. Which doesn't mean dull men are boring in bed. But they are pretty no-frills—no body paint, no themes, no kitchen floors—just straightforward, wonderful sex. Dull men never ask, "Was it good for you?" And best of all, they lack both the motivation and energy to fool around on the side. Dull men do not get—or *give*—herpes.

They are also exempted from another stylish malaise—stress. Dull men are seldom anxious. Comatose every once in a while, but never anxious. These guys have raised languor to the level of art. Give them a couch, a crossword puzzle, and a ball game and they reek of contentment.

Which is what makes them so desirable. They aren't seeking anything, they don't need to prove anything, they aren't making a statement. Dull men are terrific because they know it's OK to be regular. And like the VW, a dull guy may be a bit nondescript and none too sleek, but he is stable, holds his value, and is definitely a classic.

※

WHEN HIS SUFFERING BECOMES INSUFFERABLE

※

I wonder what the percentage is. The percentage of American women suffering from the Missing Flo Factor. Flo as in Florence Nightingale. Missing as in Totally Incapable of Ministering to Male Persons Who Are Spending the Day Home in Bed Reveling in Minor Illness and Major Helplessness.

The Missing Flo Factor—this inability to be soothing, sympathetic, or even civil toward this gentleman—is not one of the prettier aspects of our female citizenry. At some level we still labor under the dictum that the normal, womanly response to an ailing husband would be massive, lovingly dispensed doses of chicken soup and comfort. And yet when I queried a bunch of women about their compassion quotient when the old man is home ailing, most of them admitted to being less than terrific in the Nightingale department.

Typical was my friend Judy's description of the last time sickness struck her spouse. "It always starts out the same way. I vow I'm going to be wonderful and kind and attentive this time. And for the first half of the day, I am Mary Martyr. 'A little more juice, honey?' 'Today's paper, my love?' 'Shall I unplug the phone, darling?' I really do qualify for the Albert Schweitzer Sympathy and Commiseration trophy—until about one in the afternoon. Then slowly, stealthily, the true me comes out, and rage and resentment begin to fester. By the 18th time he croaks in this wimpy little voice, 'Would you mind bringing me a few more crackers?' I just HATE him.

"You can tell how my attitude alters by my stairway approach. In the morning, I'm tiptoeing up them with the grace and delicacy of Suzanne Farrell. But by five o'clock, I'm clomping down them like King Kong. I'm furious with him and even more furious at his mother who, he mournfully reminds me, would always make him tea with little cinnamon toast triangles no matter what the hour when he was sick and was-that-really-asking-too-much?"

It probably wouldn't be asking too much if women were given a chance to wallow in pathos and pain, too. But we've been trained to be the great bullet-biters of all time. Ask any doctor or nurse who the worst, most squeamish, most abysmal patients in the world are, and they're always men. Needles make them faint; close encounters of the internal kind turn them ashen; and they lean toward white-knuckled panic should blood make a personal appearance on one of their local wounds.

Women, on the other hand, are raised to be terribly stoic about These Things. We're not even allowed to scream and flail and wrench around during childbirth anymore. Dr.

Lamaze took care of all that for us. So did the pre-Lamaze generation of white-bread, knees-together, Puritan women like my friend Chris's mother, who comforted her daughter through a breech labor thusly: "Come, come, dear. I've had permanents that hurt worse. . . ."

Baby-having hurts. And one of the most educational aspects of my living abroad for six years was the chance to compare baby-having American style with baby-having Italian-style. The latter is wonderfully operatic—in Italy you can wail, you can curse, you can thrash, you can absolutely luxuriate in suffering. It is infinitely more honest to bring a child into the world amid cries of "oh, Dio mio" than to feign beatific composure to a counterfeit rhythm of pant, pant, blow.

No one denies Italian women their right to writhe in anguish, and consequently when Italian men take to their beds with a *maladia*, the Flo Factor is flowing full throttle in those Mediterranean mamas. But here in the land of the free and the home of the brave, it's really the women who seem to be the stouthearted men most of the time. Maybe if we were allowed to revel in pain a bit, then dealing with men in pain would be less of a pain.

WHEN YOUR BEST FRIENDS DIVORCE

Survival is possible. Although I would not have believed it a year ago when our best friends divorced.

Actually our connection to Carol and David transcended the sophomoric categorization of "best friends." They were family-plus, because they were family by choice, not by *fait accompli.* Family-plus because when it was Thanksgiving or Christmas we'd just say "whose house?" even though bloodline family was around the corner.

Carol is glib and verbal and David is reflective and internal and we loved them partly for mirroring those same dichotomies in our own marriage. When from time to time the chemistry had become acidic internally within one of the couples and warmth and logic choked off at an argumentative impasse, being together as a foursome seemed to loosen up the impasse and soften the harsh edges.

Only for Carol and David, the realization became more insistent that the impasses were too frequent and the chasms too profound to be circumvented with friends on the occasional evening out. And they announced their decision to break up. We weren't really surprised—but we were swamped with successive waves of sadness, then anger, then fear.

Sadness was a permissible response. Most of it was for them—for the unintentional and oblique pain they must have caused each other over the years and for the precise pain they would probably cause each other as the legal and emotional severing took place. And some of the sadness was selfish and for us. Because we were losing our mirror image partners in marital malaise. Apparently our malaise cut not much deeper than the burlesqued breast-beating of a stand-up comic, but their malaise was rooted in genuine despair.

And while we realized acknowledging that despair was the right and scary thing for them to do, we were a bit angry that they did. That anger was rather tricky to admit. But we were somewhat dependent on these two people who, by turning themselves loose in a risky and untested world, were risking our relationship with them—without even asking us. A petulant posture to be sure, but we were feeling threatened— especially during the occasional Armageddons in our own marriage when we'd mutter to ourselves that at least they had the nerve to get out . . . .

And underlying it all was the fear. The fear that we would surely lose one of them. Once the lawyers came slinking in and the acrimony quotient began to rise, signs of allegiance and support would be needed. And like the rest of the divided assets, it was logical to assume we'd ultimately become His or Hers friends.

Determined to avoid that, we made our first jagged attempts at steering through the Scylla and Charybdis course of emotional and social realignment. We were having a dinner party a month after they separated. Neither Carol nor David had plans for that night, but because Carol seemed especially down that week we asked her to join us. Because we didn't want to slight David, we invited him to dinner the night after. But our intentions of neutrality already seemed to veer off into tonal favoritism—Carol got the Saturday night soirée and David got Sunday night leftovers. Did Emily Post have a section on this?

But of course there was no right and wrong. Our mistake was the facile assumption that impartiality was rooted in tit-for-tat invitations. Carol had always adored meeting and mingling. David had always been more at ease in a quieter sort of evening. What we were doing had less to do with neutrality than with learning to reconnect with them according to their individual qualities.

Not that they weren't unique and individual before, but together they had been yin to our yang, and when their split-up shattered our cozy symbiosis, we were terrified that demi-yin would always feel half-empty. What we discovered instead, is that there is no demi-yin. Yin is fissionable, and each of them became a new and independent and complete yin while we correspondingly metamorphosed into a new yang.

And therein lay the secret of our survival. Letting go of that cramped, tidy perspective that the best they had to offer us, the most enjoyable they could be, was when they were a duo. Our resolve not to lose these two cherished people meant we had to rediscover new ways and levels of linking. I had to relate on my own to my best friend's husband without the filter of her presence or commentary. My husband could no longer deal with Carol shielded by the protective, good-ole-boy banter with David. Even the relationship between the two men had to be rewoven—wifeys weren't mutually on hand providing services of social directors.

They were unchartered, awkward months, but we all worked diligently at it. Ultimately the regrouping process afforded us all an extraordinary sense of affirmation. It was possible to fashion new meeting grounds without benefit of the convenient equation of coupledom and without letting anyone feel like a third wheel when the table was set for three.

It's very delicate territory. To survive your best friends' divorce means slogging through that initial clumsiness and reaching into resources you doubted you had. But anything less is cowardice. No one said it was easy to be modern.

MUTUAL INTERESTS DO NOT A MARRIAGE MAKE

What a curious assumption. According to a recent Merit Report survey, 50 percent of the American public thinks the most important factor in achieving a lasting relationship is for a couple to have similar interests. I must take exception. As a woman married a serious number of double-digit years, it is my heartfelt conviction that the success of any marriage is mightily bound to precisely the opposite factor—the absence of shared interests.

Show me a marriage where both partners reach for the sports section of the paper at the same time, and I'll show you a marriage on shaky ground. Show me a marriage where Wednesday nights it's duplicate bridge, Thursday nights it's a box at the symphony, and Fridays it's doubles in tennis, and I'll show you a marriage in major trouble.

It seems to me what you want in a mate is a soul who'll play yin to your yang, point to your counterpoint, George to your Gracie. What this translates to in everyday terms is that not only is it perfectly OK for her to watch Miss America and for him to watch the White Sox but that separate TV screens can be the salvation of a marriage.

Maybe it works for some people to loll about together in front of the fire and read Leo Buscaglia to each other, but for many of us, shared endeavors inevitably disrupt household harmony. Twice in my married life it was suggested to me that I take up something in order that we have some sort of mutual recreation. And those were the two times we came closest to dee-vorce: the why-don't-you-take-up-tennis time and the why-don't-you-take-up-bridge time.

Tennis was disastrous because his lack of patience and my lack of skill catapulted us from the quietude of nonintervention directly into the turbulence of catastrophic dissension: HOW COULD YOU MISS THAT SHOT?? CAN'T YOU FOLLOW THROUGH?? and sundry unprintable abuses abounded on various public courts throughout the city. We were not a pretty sight.

Bridge was even worse. That's because there were always two compatible players bearing witness to the thinly veiled domestic discord rupturing between this ostensible Charles Goren clone and his wife (whose card sense apparently had arrested prematurely at go-fish levels). Mutuality does not always a marvelous marriage make.

We're a lot smarter now. I don't take him to the ballet—that's what daughters are for anyway—and he doesn't drag me to Comiskey Park. He can pass on *Amadeus* and I can pass on wind surfing. He says no to *Sophie's Choice* and I do likewise to James Bond. Not only is it permissible, it's preferable. We each get to be experts. We have tons of new things to tell each other when we rendezvous later. I defer to him on politics and sports, and he defers to me on books and movies.

He's great on classical music, and I am superb at famous-people gossip. It's a completely satisfactory, symbiotic setup.

So I heartily disagree with 50 percent of the American public. Shared interests are what you have with your friends. Shared values are what you have with the people you marry. I'll tell you what makes a good and lasting marriage—just two little things: fundamental goodwill and the ability to laugh at the same stuff. Now how tough is that?

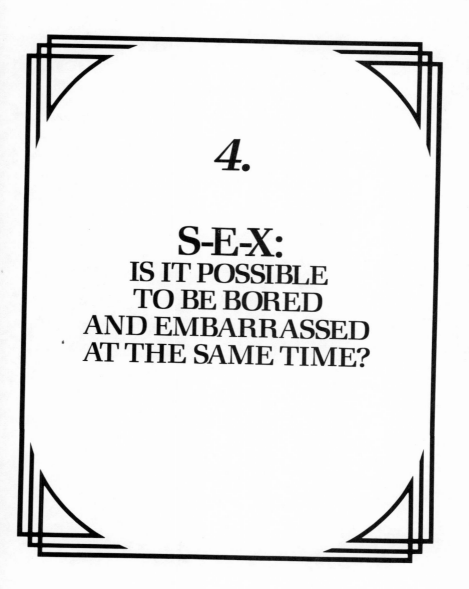

4.

S-E-X:
IS IT POSSIBLE
TO BE BORED
AND EMBARRASSED
AT THE SAME TIME?

NOW THAT MONEY HAS REPLACED SEX

This is about sex (yawn) and money (oh?) and about the many ways in which the latter seems to occupy the position of the former for women today.

Money is the last taboo. The prevalent social attitudes and mystery once rendering sex the ultimate vulgar topic, for better or worse, plague us no more. Having overdosed on sexual information and overindulged in sexual self-disclosure, the modern woman is left with but one subject firmly entrenched on the far side of bad taste—finances.

Candor in that domain is unthinkable. Money remains our last bastion of intimacy. "Are you kidding? I couldn't ask Michael what he makes," gasped my friend. Michael and said friend have been participants in a wrenching affair that's spanned three years. They've no doubt shared all the dreams, confessions, and corporal revelations indigenous to these sorts of carryings-on, and yet by mutual consent, they maintain a tacit refusal to transgress into that surviving domain of delicacy—money.

Our residual restraint about money also means we still have a wonderful opportunity to screw up our children since they've got sex all squared away, de-allured, and briskly filed. By the time they're seven they've junked their dolls equipped with privates, and they have both the anatomical and alley vocabulary to describe a full repertoire of formerly unspeakable acts.

But how will they know they're just kids, if they're not kept in the dark about something? So it's money over which we perplex and complex them. A ten-year-old asks Mommy what she makes and gets an antebellum answer like "more than $100 and less than $100,000." The point is to keep it nice and murky.

And while this mystification of money seems ludicrously misplaced, it's no more misplaced than when we were mystified about sex. Not only has money replaced sex as the primary issue shrouded in secrecy, but it is now money, not sex, women use as a touchstone for values and judgments. Were it not for money, consider the moral vacuum in which we'd exist.

Money and self-worth. A woman used to have clear-cut (albeit ill-founded) guidelines for gauging self-worth. Her self-worth used to be predicated on the sort of man who was sexually attracted to her. The past two decades have changed all of that and today even a woman with no man at her side is capable of having a sense of self-worth. And so with sexual allure now considered an invalid value system, we have adopted a new ill-founded value system. Now our self-worth is measured by our net worth. Thus the $50,000-a-year woman frequently considers herself a more accomplished and worthy human being than the woman earning $11,500. And while both working women may pay lip service to the "home manager," in their heart of hearts, it's likely that they both nurture a certain smugness because they are pulling in a paycheck.

Money, self-respect, and . . . guilt. Alongside self-worth, let us consider self-respect. In days of yore when sexual dalliances were forbidden and sexual latitude more narrowly circumscribed, it was more than clear what comprised a "self-respecting woman." That concept went up for grabs when the sexual strictures collapsed in shambles. But like a phoenix, the concept has been resurrected—this time in the financial arena.

In today's economy there is no one who doesn't respect the working woman. Except perhaps the other women who happen to carpool the self-respecting woman's offspring. So the self-respecting working woman can feel guilty for not carpooling, and the carpool mommy (self-respecting because at least she's meeting her home-front obligations) can feel guilty for not working. Thus, now that we're no longer guilty about sex, we can be real guilty about money. We're damned if we're bringing it in and damned if we aren't. A veritable hair shirt heaven.

Money and marital fireworks. Every relationship has a discord quotient that must be met. With sex defused as high-voltage fodder for marital disputes, couples have been turning increasingly to that most volatile topic—money. This is not just an imperial opinion but is the empirical observation of 400 psychiatrists who were surveyed by a medical journal. Fifty-one percent said money was the most common cause for argument—10 percent said it was sex. Quite clearly if one is looking to provoke rage or humiliation, sensibilities run deeper about the size of bank books than the size of anything else once considered pivotal to marital satisfaction. Nothing is quite so reliable for triggering domestic explosions as a tumescent Visa bill or a once-hot stock tip gone frigid.

Money and "the bottom line." The question must be posed then: now that sex no longer obsesses, confuses, or, as some might have observed, even interests us, just what does our rising money consciousness mean? Perhaps it is still too early to tell. And yet one can't help but be struck by the feeling that in order not to appear like a bimbo, today's woman has indiscriminately opted for bullish. "Money is power" and all that sounds very realistic, but also a bit reverential. And it makes you wonder whether we just freed ourselves of one manipulative myth and simultaneously bought into another.

IF ONLY YOU COULD FORGET THAT FIRST TIME

The annual orgy of Beatle nostalgia just might put Rosie away. The last parlor game in the world Rosie ever wanted to play was: "Do you remember 20 years ago tonight when the Beatles were on Ed Sullivan?"

How could Rosie forget? She remembers exactly what was going on in her life on February 9, 1964, at 7:00 P.M. Central Standard Time. She was losing her virginity in a bunk bed on the third floor of a Big Ten fraternity house.

At the very moment 70 million people in living rooms across America were being swept away by John, Paul, George, and Ringo, Rosie was in a bedroom giving it away to Harvey.

It was not what she had planned to do that evening. She had planned, like the rest of the immediate world, to be glued to her TV screen. Instead she was glued to Harvey.

And she wishes more than anything that she'd chosen almost any other time than that time for her first time.

It is not any solace to Rosie that almost everyone has a less-than-wonderful first time. First times aren't meant to be wonderful. They are only meant to be gotten over with so you can get on with the second and third time and start working your way toward wonderful. Rosie probably could have gotten over this less-than-wonderful moment a lot more gracefully if the entire world hadn't chosen to stop dead in its tracks and canonize this particular evening as if it were the cultural turning point of the entire 20th century.

How would you feel if you'd spent 19 years doggedly guarding your virtue and then the one night you choose to finally give it up is commemorated on an annual basis by every TV and radio station in the country over the next 20 years? It's doubtful anyone over the age of 25 can remember back to the actual date when they first Did It.

The surroundings you can remember, the awkwardness

you can remember, the name of your partner you can even remember, but the calendar date? Not a chance. Great cocktail repartee almost never includes a suggested icebreaker like "Did you know that I started Doing It eight years ago today?" But Rosie never had a chance to forget February 9, 1964.

Not when on February 9 everybody was squealing and raving about the bouncy, British boychicks who'd just been on TV. And the "Oh, Rosie, didn't you think they were darling?" inquiries made it somewhat difficult to say, "I didn't get a chance to see them," without sounding like a cultural cripple. Not seen them? What could have been more important for Rosie to do that Sunday than seeing the Beatles? Only unloading her virginity.

So there was Rosie nurturing a dual sense of deprivation. Not only had she managed to miss out on seeing the Beatles, but she also had managed to miss out on the supposed "and the earth moved" moment promised in her well-thumbed *Love without Fear* manual.

For those who were not around then, in 1964 it was still believed that every time you Did It—if you Did It Right—"the earth moved."

What Rosie felt was not even a quiver of terra firma. What Rosie felt in the frat house bunk bed was simply the standard response to the overly anticipated seduction—an overwhelming urge to sing "Is That All There Is?"

Meanwhile, everyone else was singing snippets of "I Want to Hold Your Hand" and other yeah, yeah, yeah ditties. Rosie, not immune to life's cruel ironies, was not particularly thrilled that the entire country seemed to be suffused in songs of innocence on the very night that she had said *ciao* to hers.

And unlike most of us, who are permitted to forget our ignominious initiation into the intricacies of intercourse, Rosie is being forced yet again to remember hers as we flog ourselves into a frenzy of phony nostalgia over February 9, 1964.

Rosie just wishes they'd let it be, let it be.

WHEN BALD MEN BEGIN
TO LOOK GOOD TO YOU

Millions of hours, millions of dollars, and millions of dashed hopes later, millions of men still remain irrevocably bald. Assuming these men are aware of the inherent (no pun intended) hyperbole in the biblical tale of Samson and his locks, what causes them to perceive naked skulldom as so shameful?

They seem to be unapprised of some rather significant Sex Appeal statistics: a 1982 study revealed 60 percent of the female population feels bald men aren't much different in the S.A. department than gentlemen with abundant tresses; and a full 6 percent frequently find the tressless even more appealing than their furry-topped counterparts. I am in fact a 6 percenter, and to assuage the anxiety of you men blessed with something less than plush plumage, I'd like to speak on behalf of the 66 percent of us who do not feel the hairless are handicapped.

First of all, I admit to harboring a bias. I personally feel there is no man on the face of this earth—Tom Selleck, Richard Gere, and Robert (reverential hush) Redford included—who does not appear monumentally effete with a blow dryer in hand. Take away the need for a blow dryer and already you have made three giant steps forward in Markey's Measurement of Manliness Manual.

Second, I feel the rubbing on of pathetically impotent potions, the weaving in of phony filaments, the grafting on of furry flaps, and the punching in of painful plugs all catapult an otherwise respectable man directly into the arena of high wimpdom. Ultra-wimpdom is almost always achieved, however, by those who opt for the inevitably tawdry toupee. No matter the expertise, no matter the expense, there isn't a toupee around that befools when worn in a horizontal situation. The extremes you men will go to.

Extremes such as (wince) castration or emasculation. Yes, these rather drastic procedures are indeed guaranteed preventive measures of baldness. A classic study has been made involving identical male twins. One had been inadvertently (it is hoped) emasculated before reaching puberty—and certainly must have wrestled with a severe case of sibling rivalry. However (and who says there's no justice?), when the twins turned 20, baldness blighted the otherwise fully equipped member of twindom, while curly locks still bedecked the memberless member.

So, keeping in mind the old architectural axiom "less is more," here comes the question: Which twin would most women choose as their companion on a desert island? The one with or the one without the Toni? Granted the choice is hypothetical, but pertinent if we are to put baldness into perspective. After all, there are deficiencies and there are deficiencies.

And who says baldness is a deficiency? Like many of life's little vagaries, baldness offers a man an incredible opportunity for character building. For starters he develops a sensational sense of humor. Taunted by cheap shots, such as "Hey, bowling-ball brain," he is forced to either (a) skin and bare it (sorry) or (b) toss back rapier-wit retorts such as "Grass doesn't grow on a busy street, fella." Look at our society's most outrageous clowns: Woody Allen, Bob Newhart . . . James Watt. All of them have serious scalp visibility.

Additionally, a bald man nurtures an endearing sense of optimism. These guys never toss out the old brush and comb. It's hard not to be enchanted by a man who holds fast to his dream. And last, there's the implicit honesty of a man whose integrity won't permit him to indulge in the pathetic ploys of any hair-raising cover-ups.

Gentlemen, for 66 percent of us, you are wasting your time, your money, and your anguish. What sort of a woman falls for a man with a full head of hair? Nancy Reagan, that's who. If you want a woman with a little more edge than that, just polish up that smoothly rounded pate of yours, honey, and let it shine, let it shine.

✳

INFIDELITY: DO YOU REALLY WANT TO KNOW?

✳

I am about to take what is surely a minority viewpoint on the ever-popular subject of marital infidelity. It is not a pro position or a con position. It's an awareness position. My stand on infidelity is the old head-in-the-sand posture—I do not want to know. I do not want to be confessed to during some sloppy remorse-filled moment, because I figure if a person is going to open up his life to extra craziness, then he should be ready to deal with the extra craziness all on his grown-up own. And I certainly do not want to be so crazed and suspicious myself that I would resort to sleuthing around to nail someone in *flagrante delicto*. To what end?

That was the question that riddled my innards as I listened to Ron and Gigi Moers explain the crafty ensnarement techniques taught by their Wives Infidelity Service, a little do-it-yourself detective business they set up in the benign environs of Schaumburg, Illinois, where apparently some wives thought there was a bit of extracurricular bedroom behavior going on that wasn't benign at all.

It's interesting to note from a recent Merit Report that though most people think more than half the married population is screwing around, when it comes to their own personal home, only 7 percent have ever seriously suspected their personal spouse of sexual dalliance. The old it-could-never-happen-to-me syndrome trips into high gear when it comes to cuckolding. But Wives Infidelity Service apparently has found that 7 percent market.

They offer a five-week course to teach women how to run their very own investigation. We're talking bugging phones, logging exits, walkie-talkies, and a nifty, nefarious device that kicks on a tape recorder should a mattress become busy at an unusual hour of the day. We're talking high drama and major confrontation.

What could possibly be served by waving some Mr. and Mrs. motel receipts in front of the old man and saying in a rational adult voice (because Wives Infidelity Service cautions you not to say "Gotcha, you s.o.b."), "I think we ought to talk about this"? Wouldn't it be better *not* to talk about it? I mean if he basically has been there at the dinner table with you for 14 years and is still warm and loving and you've woven a life together with kids and dogs and mortgages and history, why on earth would you want to confront him with what might be only a momentary indiscretion?

I said "might." There are affairs and there are affairs. There are momentary indiscretions and there are ultimate betrayals, and what they are labeled often has less to do with the affair itself than the attitude of the affair participant's spouse. I don't see the point of putting a 14-year marriage on the line because of a limited relationship that usually has a beginning, a middle, and an end. This kind of conjugal confrontation only stirs up all sorts of contrition, regrets, misunderstandings, and all those swell emotions that keep resurfacing to leach the last vestiges of good feelings from a marriage. Unless you're looking to exit from the marriage in a swirl of self-righteousness, isn't it better to take a pass on playing private eye?

Fifty percent of the Moerses' clients get divorced, and half of those who remain married stay only because they're financially locked in. Which means only 25 percent of those who thought they wanted to know, and now know, even have a chance of a happy ending.

The Moerses say most women go the Sam Spade route because they want leverage, and they want to know what they're up against. Well, what they're going to be up against isn't the bimbo he's bedding, it's the bitter aftertaste of a confirmed infidelity that haunts them as they go through the motions of trying to reconstruct something from the rubble of their confrontation.

As far as infidelity goes, ignorance may not be bliss, but it's definitely preferable to knowledge—when you're going to use that knowledge to destroy something that probably is well worth saving.

$$\ast$$

WHEN YOUR SEXUAL CONSCIOUSNESS REFUSES TO BE RAISED

$$\ast$$

This is for all you women, who, like me, thought you were sexually repressed after going to one of Those Parties. You know, those gatherings where the goods on display fall somewhere between Fredericks of Hollywood lingerie and soft-core whips and chains. The purveying of these exotic wares in the privacy of both urban and suburban living rooms began to proliferate a few years ago when some very savvy marketing folk decided to cross-breed erotica with respectability. This, of course, segued perfectly with the media barrage from Hite, Reuben, Kassorla, et al, who've done their best over the past decade to boost the carnal-consciousness quotient of the female populace.

We've been browbeaten with choruses of whatever turns you on, any woman can, and nice girls do. Yet even though our sexual mindset has been forcibly expanded, there still aren't many Nike-soled females who can be induced into serious, thoughtful perusing at the local sex shop. Sex shops are still viewed as predominantly the domain of pervs and fringe societal types. And back-of-the-book ads and plain brown wrappers quite clearly have only scratched the surface of our paraphernalia purchasing potential. So Those Parties were set up to reach all these women supposedly anxious to explore these recently legitimized aphrodisiac alternatives.

For starters, our sexually integrated hostess plied us with some domestic vino until the pitch person came to unpack her dubious wares on the dining room table. Then, when everyone felt safe, communally naughty, and assuredly receptive, the gadgetry gala got on its way rather spectacularly. Renee, the sexwares sales rep, welcomed us and then called in her assistant Eric to pass out small favors. Leaping into the room like cupid incarnate was a rather scantily clad male person attired in your basic silver jock strap (the metallic look being so fashionable last fall) with a jaunty matching mask. Eric's appearance was surely an attempt to dissipate any shreds of middle class embarrassment we may have harbored. At the sight of Eric *presque au naturel*, women raised on *Gone with the Wind* and wafty Johnny Mathis ballads were supposed to metamorphose into born-again voluptuaries. Admittedly he did elicit squeals of delight from the gathered females as he proceeded to hand out prosaically normal number 2 pencils with explicitly phallic erasers. The evening proceeded tastefully from there.

Next came the soft wear—items called Risqué, Lacy Nothing, Sheer Delight, and Paramour—all black and red variants of the standard cutout and peekaboo theme. But while everybody oohed and ahhed as the frothy wisps were presented, there were two somewhat negative forces at work preventing these items from being big sellers. First of all, the majority of women at this party happened to be nurses—obstetric/gynecological nurses, no less—and even they, women not prone to feigning anatomical modesty, had enormous difficulty as the limp undie ensembles were passed about figuring out what went where, what stayed coyly covered, and what did not. What did not had a great deal to do with negative force number two. The bulk of us were something less (actually something more) than conventional centerfold material. Our souls may have been Bo Derek, but our bodies were dumpy, and when it came to draping these bodies with little more than feathers and rhinestone garter belts, very few of us were willing to take the plunge.

What we did opt for were some of the more benign potions and gels. "Emotion Lotion" (come on, don't laugh), a heat-generating balm, was a big mover in both cherry and banana flavors. Whether its appeal was based on our erotic or our arthritic proclivities, no one hazarded a confession.

(Apropos of arthritis, it must be mentioned that one of the party participants came with her mother. Mom was in fact a member of the cane-carrying, bifocaled generation whose concerns one once assumed might be centered on church suppers, bingo, and prize-winning dahlias. Evidently this Mom was a bit feistier than that, because there was no one who laughed more boisterously or filled out her order form more rapidly than did this lady. The mind-boggling thing about it, aside from wondering what Dad was like, was that she and her daughter filled out the form together. For me it was the most scandalous part of the evening. *My Mother/My Self* notwithstanding, there are still a lot of us otherwise liberated ladies who in our heart of hearts remain convinced Mom never Did It and even if she did, certainly not with enthusiasm or devices. So much for sociological sidebars.)

The finale, of course, was the Cuisinart of the boudoir—those myriad versions of vibrating appendages that are supposedly *de rigueur* for the sexually chic set. Batteries, plugs, attachments, and multiple whatevers were passed about and openly marveled at. When the top-of-the-line model, formidable in size and rife with options, made the rounds, one nurse staged a swoon and gasped, "My God, I've fallen in love!"

That's when Renee came in for the kill. Order forms were

passed out and it was real hard not to feel like Mary Poppins if you didn't buy at least $30 of obligatory kinkiness. But I couldn't. It was beginning to dawn on me that I'd just been victimized by the ultimately intrusive hype—some genius had just parlayed addictive American consumerism out of the kitchen into the bedroom and tried to make me feel that no-frills sex was fraught with obsolescence. I crumpled up my order form and went home. The way I figured it, if it was good enough for Eve to get kicked out of the Garden, it's still good enough for me.

NAME THE PARTS: THE GAME YOU STILL CAN'T MASTER

It's got to be pretty blushy stuff to get old Phil Donahue embarrassed. I mean, this is the guy who has routinely hosted shows on some pretty warped topics, and while he is frequently uncomfortable (and sometimes aghast) in the presence of some of the sideshow citizenry who are his guests, one is hard put to recall the last time Mr. D. went crimson.

But he was undone by "Humanopoly"—an oh-so-biologically accurate board game designed for parents who are in the process of . . . *gulp* . . . educating their kids about *s-e-x*.

Mr. D. actually did a remarkable job of maintaining a decorous demeanor throughout the opening moves, like choosing whether he wanted to be a sperm or an egg, and then tossing the dice to start his trek down the old fallopian tubes. But when he had to draw a "love" card and read its contents over the nationally syndicated air waves, the big blush nailed him. Poor Phil. He had drawn a card that had some of Those Words. Those awful, anatomically correct, but appalling-to-articulate words that most of us would only rather die than have to say in forums either public or private.

The truth is, no matter how progressive you are in your at-home educational program, the ickiest aspect is never explaining the processes—it's naming the parts. Somehow even those of us who are committed to sexual enlightenment, and are otherwise linguistically liberated, still have to force ourselves not to regress into sexual pseudonyms.

Of course if you think about it, sexual pseudonyms are ultimately charged with more mortification and blush potential than sexual straight talk ever could be. Remember the classic scene in *Bob and Carol and Ted and Alice* where Dyan Cannon is telling her shrink how her eight-year-old son had recently inquired why daddies have a wiffle and mommies have a tee-tee? The shrink did not deal gracefully with wiffle and tee-tee.

And wiffle and tee-tee aren't the worst of it. In their recent book, *Children's Sexual Thinking*, Ronald and Juliette Goldman presented a list of commonplace, adorable euphemisms children are currently spouting in lieu of the nouns in *Gray's Anatomy*. We have "kiki," "dingle," "thing-a-ma-jig," and—are you ready for this?—"gentiles."

It's hard to believe it's the 1980s when you think about the creative contortions many of us are still going through to avoid dealing with Those Words. Back in the days when we were 21 and making major proclamations that when we were grown-ups we'd be nothing less than the perfect parents, didn't most of us make a real commitment to clinical candor? So how come we continue to go all clammy and smirky when it's terminology time? How come no matter how poised we are, none of us can say the word *placenta* without spending the next 30 seconds getting our gag reflex under control?

Surely the kids pick up on our queasiness quotient, and it's probably a major reason they take a quantum leap directly into four-letter phraseology. Conceivably if we could break through some of our residual remorse, the nine-year-olds would have less reason to embrace all the hardcore expletives of which they have such a thorough working knowledge these days. Who knows? But how can we ever expect the future sexually active citizens of America to feel comfortable about their bodies and all the bodily options if we're still feeling dopey about articulating the routine anatomical terms?

Maybe I'm wrong. Maybe it's still more *our* problem than *theirs.* I draw this conclusion only because of the sibling altercation overheard at the school bus stop. Ten-year-old Beth was being taunted by her seven-year-old brother Terry that someday *soon* she was going to have "boobies."

With immense élan and incredible exasperation, Beth placed her hand on her as-yet-hipless hip and sighed, "Breasts, Terry. Breasts."

Maybe there's hope.

DOOMED TO BE SEXUALLY UNCHIC

I am doomed to be sexually unchic. When free love was the rage in my home state of California, I was going to a midwestern university that had curfews for "coeds" and was filled with "coeds" who wouldn't consider the Pill until their mother's gynecologist prescribed it six weeks before their wedding. When bisexuality became an option, I'd gotten used to men, and the women I met were all in various stages of sequential pregnancy, like me. When vibrators and other electronic wizardry became standard accoutrements in America's boudoirs, I was living in Europe, where life moves at 220 volts, and all our transformers were in the kitchen.

And now this. Two new sexual phenomena are sweeping the land and neither of them is going to work for me. The first is Inhibited Sexual Desire. ISD is jargon for a total lack of interest in all things sexual, and several sexologists say it affects about 20 percent of the population.

I think I had ISD for years, when the littlest Markeys were insomniacs, bed-wetters and nightmare-sufferers. When days started at 5:30 A.M. and ended at 1:00 A.M. and were strewn with Legos and laundry, and the little darlings never held up their end of the conversation other than to ask "Why?" 72 times an hour. As far as I was concerned during those years, beds were for nothing more vigorous than passing out on, although Masters and Johnson and Nancy Friday were busy pontificating about the unplumbed depths of the American woman's lust. My as-yet-undubbed ISD and I felt terribly aberrant, so I was immensely relieved, when my offsprings' needs diminished, to see that my sexual needs increased.

It was just like getting back on a bike—you never do forget. And as a second-time-around sybarite, you're capable of wonderful refinement. In fact, I've been busy refining myself right into my much-read-about peak years. Here I am, primed for optimum performance, and what do they do but ISD me into obsolescence.

The second thing I'm missing out on is ear sex. Ear sex actually is linked to ISD because it's a substitute for a real sexual encounter. Ear sex consists of paying to have someone call you up and talk dirty while you listen or do whatever people do while being telephonically titillated. Ear sex has brought new meaning to the reach-out-and-touch-someone concept and has done wonders for sales on both cordless and speaker phones. It does seem a bit warped, but given the convenience, anonymity, and herpes-free aspects, you can understand how it has become something of a logical alternative to The Real Thing.

And, since ISD has rendered The Real Thing no longer in vogue, I would like a crack at being sexually *au courant* by at least trying ear sex. Nothing too hard-core, mind you, but I wouldn't mind if some Kris Kristofferson-like voice whispered a few endearments to me on my white Princess Trimline. The problem is, I never have access to my white Princess Trimline because the ISD instigators/Lego lovers/"Why?" whiners of yesteryear are now teenagers-in-training. I can barely get a car-pool call in, much less one that might appeal to my prurient interests.

The obvious solution would be to get call-waiting, but I consider that even more morally objectionable than ear sex. Besides, given my timing in the sexual domain, the outcome would be inevitable:

Kris K: "And then I'm going to [bleep] your [bleep], and. . . ."

Me (pant, pant): "Oooooh. . . ."

CLICK

Me: "Uh, could you [pant] hold on for one second?"

CLICK: "Hello? Oh, hi, Mother."

Doomed, I tell you.

5.

THE WONDROUS AND WRENCHING LESSONS OF PARENTHOOD

BE CAREFUL WHAT YOU WISH FOR

It was clearly a case of "be careful what you wish for. . . . You might get it." Like any working mother, one thing I've always wished for was a chance to be in my own home deliciously alone for an entire evening. When you live in the thick of a bustling family, solitude in the cocoony comforts of home is a hard commodity to come by.

I've often envied my good friend, who lives alone in the peace and fingerprintless finery of her high-rise condo. Said friend regularly journeys forth to spend weekends in the midst of our standard tribal din and usually departs with raging four-star headaches. And when she leaves, I always fantasize what it would be like to retreat into Garboesque reclusiveness and indulge myself in the sumptuous luxury of aloneness.

Here's the be-careful-what-you-wish-for-you-might-get-it part. Last weekend, my solitude scenario serendipitously fell into place—father and son had a major camping expedition, and the almost-adolescent had a pajama party.

Visions of silken serenity began to dance in my head. I could read Jane Eyre or Barbara Cartland; I could write

105

bunches of letters or read through bundles of old ones; I could play Berlioz or Bette Midler; I could dine on chips and Coke or cold lobster and champagne. I could sculpt the entire evening according to whim, without taking into consideration either the presence or preferences of any other person. Extraordinarily exhilarating.

And also extraordinarily scary. Because as the weekend grew closer, I began to question my atrophied abilities to savor the sensations of solitude. Suppose I blew the entire evening and restlessly wandered about, hacking away at a Sara Lee chocolate swirl cake, dabbling over a third of the crossword puzzle, flicking the TV on and off in disgust. Doing one of everything, winding up having accomplished nothing, and all this flailing activity no more than a frenetic ruse to avoid the main event: the experience of By Myselfness.

The French have a wonderful expression—*être bien dans sa peau*, which literally translated means "to be well in one's skin." What it really means is to be comfortable, integrated, and generally pleased to be yourself. Confronted with my first evening in years of unstructured at-home isolation, it was clear that I and my *peau* might have a way to go before we really establish any sort of peaceful coexistence.

Twenty-five percent of the American population lives alone full time. How do they do it—out of inner harmony or enforced habit? Was I so vapid, were my inner resources so undeveloped, that I was already writhing at the prospect of a 15-hour mini-stint? We all aspire to be moderately engaging human beings, but like the old if-a-tree-falls-in-the-forest-and-no-one-is-there-to-hear-it inquiry, if there is no one there to perceive how engaging we might be, how engaging are we?

I know how to read. I know how to think. But husband and children and the inherent compromises and fragmentation of daily family life have provided a convenient distraction and a protective haven from actually doing either on an extended basis. And bereft of the obstacles I loved to complain about, one dose of Saturday night solitude was beginning to feel as insurmountable a challenge as one week on a godforsaken mountaintop courtesy of Outward Bound.

And so, as the week progressed, I chafed and fretted but remained fiercely determined to tough it out, and to . . . ringgggg. You guessed it. Divine intervention came on Thursday. An old friend from Paris was in for the weekend and wanted to go to George's to hear *le jazz*.

So I got *le jazz* instead of *le solitude*. I know it was just a temporary reprieve, but it sure felt great to break through the Greta myth and acknowledge the truth: I don't vant to be alone at all. Just give me constant chaos and cacophony to kvetch about, and I'll be a happy woman.

BEING TOTALLY RESPONSIBLE FOR THE SEXUAL ENLIGHTENMENT OF MINORS

So here come Ronald and Juliette Goldman—a sort of Masters and Johnson for kiddies—with this guaranteed-to-be-talk-show-fodder book called *Children's Sexual Thinking*. It is crammed with enough appalling findings about our children's perceptions of s-e-x to unnerve even the most resolutely enlightened household sexual educators.

The appalling finding that will get the most media play is that American kids are sexually ignorant compared with their Swedish, English, and Australian peers. But the appalling finding that outrankles that is this: Most children get their sexual education from their mothers, their teachers, or the media. In that order. Most of them have *no confidence* in asking their fathers about sex.

Oh, swell. How is it that daddies are exempt from yet another domestic charge? I can see pre-pubescent girls dodging Dad and coming to Mom with their anatomical que-ries and pre-menstrual perturbances. But Dad's credibility/ knowledgeability/accessibility rating is so low that the boys are coming to Mom, too.

God knows most of us—male and female alike—have done our best to crash through the double-messaged sexual tutel-age of the "Fabulous Fifties" (It's natural, it's wonderful, don't you dare do it until you're married.") and emerge as sexually integrated grown-ups. But apparently a well-aimed inquiry from a curious offspring rattles men's sexual cohesiveness even more than women's. Thus, no matter how liberated the household, just as laundry-folding has stayed predominantly in the female domain, so has the responsibility for sexual elucidation.

I know this is true because of the following story. This spring my friend Janice was innocently at work in the quasi-frozen tundra of her garden when her son and his best buddy came crashing outside, shoving each other forward and getting as close to giggling as regulation 12-year-old boys get.

Janice adopted her most modulated, mature, matter-of-fact voice. "Go on, boys, I know it's about sex. It's fine to ask me; there's nothing to be embarrassed about."

And faster than you can say cardiac arrest, her son plunged in: "Mom, what's 'coming'?"

She did her best. As Janice tells it, they were seeking both male and female definitions. As Janice tells it, it was a whole lot easier to explain the male version because it was only in the past few years that she'd figured out the female version. As Janice tells it, there wasn't enough wine in the world to get her through the rest of the afternoon. As Janice tells it, Mr. Janice was asleep in front of the TV through the entire intimate inquisition, and his only response to her magical moment of parenthood was to roll his eyes, gulp, and tell her she "handled" it real well.

Why don't dads ever "handle" it? I asked a few of them and their general response was, "harumph, harumph, well, I have a tacit understanding with the kids that they can always come to me if they have any questions. . . ."

Like true-and-false or multiple-choice? What about sexual

values and attitudes and all the nuances that make sexual awareness a lot more than a compendium of facts and positions? The Goldman studies indicate that boys are especially susceptible to misinformation—by the time they are teenagers, fewer than half feel comfortable asking their mothers and fewer than one-quarter feel comfortable asking their fathers. So, whom can they ask?

Listen, gentlemen, you have got to leap into the information breach. So you stumble a bit, or blush, and try to quell your own regressive peculiarities. Your kid isn't looking for any definitive declamation. A little dialogue will do, for starters.

BOREDOM: THE ULTIMATE TERROR

The hostess to a French couple visiting the United States was pointing out some of the wondrous highlights of *la vie Américaine*. "Here's the town pool, and the town tennis complex, and here is where we ice skate. Here is where the children take their ceramic course, and their tap-dancing and gymnastic lessons. And on Saturday they play soccer here. . . . It's really a terrific place to live, don't you think?"

"*C'est extraordinaire*," replied the Parisienne with all the Gallic grace she could muster, "but in America, boredom, it is forbidden?"

Whether boredom is a right we've been denied or an art we've lost, the very mention of it strikes almost as much cold terror in our hearts as herpes simplex. Heaven forbid we should leave ourselves—or, even worse, our children—face-to-face with an unscheduled chunk of time after school, on a weekend or during vacation.

As mothers ran into each other during those last precious weeks of school, a communal sense of desperation underscored their more-than-conversational curiosity when they asked, "What's Johnny doing this summer?" And woe to the child who wasn't scheduled up.

Summer used to be lazy, unfocused days loosely linked around swimming, biking, or a neighborhood ball game. Try to hustle up an impromptu ball game in the summer these days and, even though budgets may be tight, 98 percent of the neighborhood kids will be enrolled in some sort of organized activity—summer school, private camp, or a local park district program.

The park district brochure in my mailbox two months ago offered a cornucopia of diversion from "Aerobic Swimmer-cise" to "Videotaped Golf Lessons" to the *pièce de résistance*—a nine-week course with the eerie title "Explore and Create." Explore and create is exactly what would take place if we'd stop signing the kids up and let them fend for themselves through the limp and leaden days of summer.

Listen, I'm not a masochist. I cherish as much as the next woman the sound of little children crashing out the door with a "See ya later, Mom," and a sack lunch in hand, heading for an entire day of all-in-good-fun supervised activities. It's certainly a more convenient prospect than a day punctuated by 87 in-and-out door slams and the incessant, irksome inquiries: "Have you seen my mitt?" or "Can Harold come over?" or "Is there any lemonade?"

But there's a price to be paid for our uninterrupted, door-slamless days, and more than anyone it's our kids who are paying it. Their chances to develop any resourcefulness are increasingly choked off as the labyrinth of planned events grows more and more dense. A significant dose of some good old-fashioned languor would do wonders to nurture some inventiveness and self-reliance.

Know any kids who have spent an afternoon writing a poem or orchestrating a puppet show? Probably not. The only verses or dramas being generated by the younger-than-13-year-old-set these days are those wrung from classes with names like "Rhyme Time" and "The Play's the Thing." I know a kid who was incredulous to discover that his dog could swim without the benefit of lessons.

And I know a man who is so appalled by his son's perception of baseball as an organized sport to be played only by a computer-selected team, at a specific hour, while wearing $25 uniforms, that he is planning to build a gritty city alley behind his manicured subdivision colonial and place his son and his cronies there for an entire summer. He'll give them some busted equipment, some garbage pails for rummaging, and some stoops for serious sitting. He's convinced once they get the hang of it they'll revel in the rapture of unstructured days.

The only problem he anticipates is luring them back there, but he has figured out the perfect solution. He's listing it in next year's park district brochure: "Alley Amusements: Learning the Art of Aimlessness."

I've already signed my kid up.

NONSEXIST NOTIONS: A SUCCESS STORY

I just hadn't planned to fail in this area, too. Though it's true I never stopped shaving my legs or became a card-carrying member of any consciousness-raising group, I'd always fancied myself resoundingly liberated and certainly capable of rearing two children in a nonsexist environment. And if it was clear after the first decade that I hadn't succeeded in turning out perfect free-to-be-you-and-me specimens, I'd at least given it my best shot and neither son nor daughter would disgrace me if marooned on an island with Gloria Steinem or Phil Donahue.

But in two unrelated incidents starring my supposedly enlightened, non-gender-stereotyped offspring, it became clear I evidently had made a few detours from liberation lane.

The eight-year-old son: Though his room has a plethora of Matchbox cars and GI Joe paraphernalia, he also possessed (until last year) a few frowsy dolls and to this day is perfectly comfortable sleeping with a teddy bear. He enthusiastically acknowledges some of the best players on his soccer team are irreversibly female; he delights in any sort of baking; he vacuums his room; and he has made several major attempts at sewing. A regular Alan Alda.

Not so fast, Ms. Miracle of Modern Motherhood. How was I to know that lurking inside this sensitive househusband-in-training was a lecherous M.C.P. about to burst forth? But, I can tell you, my heart froze when he inquired, "Mom, can I see your *Playboy?*"

OK, OK. I know what you're saying. If I'm going for the Letty Cottin Pogrebin Non-Sexist Child Rearing Award, what is *Playboy* doing in my home? There is only one answer: Rita Jenrette. Who could resist buying *that* issue? Anyway, the eight-year-old knew that particular issue was on the premises, and he was real interested in a little prurient perusal. I knew it was prurient, because he's still reading *Fox in Sox,* so there were no pretensions that he only wanted it for the interview.

I knew exactly why he wanted it, exactly how exploitative some of its photos were, and exactly how repressive I'd sound if I said no. I didn't want him to think I thought women's bodies were Dirty, so when I said yes, I tried to explain in precise eight-year-old terms the difference between looking and leering at the female form. This speech was something of a hybrid between Mr. Rogers and Germaine Greer, but I assumed the message got through and felt smugly convinced I'd not raised a libidinous leprechaun. Wrong.

Peacock-proud, he dragged me into his room an hour later. Gone were the 17 posters of cuddly, androgynous E.T., and in their stead were the airbrushed, pulchritudinous wonders his lascivious little fingers had just ripped out of the magazine. Was I back to square one? "Gosh, Mom, do you believe the boobs on that one!" Square one it was.

The 12-year-old daughter: The child spent the first decade of her life in overalls, received a baseball mitt when she was six, never liked dolls, and, other than her ballet shoes, has never owned a pink anything. There's just nothing girly-girly about her.

Or so I thought until I read the last chapter of her recently assigned autobiography. "Future Ambitions" began admirably enough with aspirations toward a career in medicine, computers, or law, but then came the clincher: "One thing that I really want is to get married to a rich, handsome, charming man, live in the suburbs, and have two children—one boy and one girl." I was devastated. Years and years spent combatting the simpering stereotype, and here it is in black and white—I've reared a mini-Marabelle Morgan.

"How could you?" I rail. "Is that really your goal in life?"

"Oh, Mom, don't blow a spas. My only goal was to fill up space, because it had to be eight pages long."

Relief shudders through me. "So all that about marriage, the suburbs, a boy and a girl aren't your goals in life?"

"Of course not. It's perfectly OK if I have two girls."

Square zero.

❊

SAYING GOODBYE TO
MORE THAN HALLOWEEN

❊

It wasn't just Halloween we said goodbye to that fall of '82. When the Tylenol tragedy struck and armies of moms and dads screeched to a halt and said "not this year" to trick-or-treat plans, some said we overreacted and others made apocalyptical statements about the night that Halloween died. But it seems many of us might be missing the point.

When I bribed my seven-year-old with ten dollars to stay home, I wasn't simply bidding farewell to that kiddy costume holiday. I was giving in to an awareness of menace and fragility that until now had seemed beyond the scope of American perceptions.

I was convinced years ago, after living in Europe where everyone my age nurtured some nugget of horrific personal tragedy from the war, that "those people" really knew what life was about. Our native myopia and naiveté struck me as insufferably smug and less than admirable.

But now that naiveté has been bludgeoned to death—its demise not triggered by the cataclysmic bloodletting and bombing of wartime, but by the steady erosion of our sense of serenity that's taken place over the last 20 years. Mutilated pelicans, poisoned medications, random anonymous street violence, and assassination attempts as regular as clockwork have wreaked havoc with the set of assumptions I'd hoped to pass on to my children.

Basic assumptions not only of decency and law and order, but also the assumptions of personal freedom indigenous to our society. My sense of personal freedom is feeling very battered these days. I feel myself acquiescing to an elusive, free-floating sense of peril. A sense of peril no longer restricted to the historical domain of world powers and politics, but one that has insidiously worked its way into my home, and certainly transcends trick-or-treat.

Our version of Halloween was always a bit aberrant anyway—metamorphosed from All Saints Day into a masquerade, an orgy of sweets, and relatively benign threats of pranks. So saying goodbye to Halloween isn't killing me.

What's killing me is the feeling that I would have been tacitly courting disaster if I hadn't said goodbye. What's killing me is that some wackos out there were manipulating my once-innocent decisions about Tootsie Rolls and Listerine. What's killing me is that those same wackos are the reason my son turned to me last week offering the following advice about whom I should vote for in the next election: "What you do, Mom, is vote for the bad guy. That way, someone will shoot him, and he'll be dead." That is my seven-year-old's view of the world—delivered with the same absence of perturbance with which he explains the rules of second-grade soccer.

So it's happened. Our children's gut acceptance about this world's chaos potential is pretty close to that of the Europeans whose life awareness I so admired. What I didn't see through the romantic haze of admiration for that awareness was its nasty flipside. When the awareness of the craziness out there seeps in and you get a little crazed too. When you get a little further removed from the possibility of joyous or abandoned participation in life. When you get cautious and risk being crippled by your caution and you sound more and more like John Irving's Garp warning the kids to beware of the undertoad. Where the line between prudence and paranoia is no longer clear.

YOUR FIRST
NO-SANTA-CLAUS CHRISTMAS

This was our first middle-aged Christmas. The first one where there was no Santa Claus. Not a believer in the house. It sure made things a bit flattened out. Not empty, not hollow, but a little echo-y and a whole lot different.

S.C. bit the dust last September in tandem with the Tooth Fairy. At the Moment of Truth I only remember feeling relieved. Relieved on the Tooth Fairy front to no longer have to remember after coming home late from the movies to soundlessly slip a few sous under the pillow and leave no telltale evidence. (My brother never forgave my mom for leaving some giveaway gloves behind.)

Relieved on the Santa Claus front to no longer have to remember to wrap the Santa presents in different paper from the Mom and Dad presents. Relieved to no longer have to write all the "From Santa" gift tags with my shaky, illegible left hand. Relieved to no longer have to obtain the services of an unfamiliar-voiced office colleague to be our own personal Santa to ho-ho-ho on the phone when our kids called in their list. (Somehow they always knew the multiple department store St. Nicks were shabby counterfeits.)

So in September we were relieved. And the shortest person in the family who'd kept us plugged into the fiction for years was kind of thrilled and proud. He'd just stepped into the insiders' circle. On one hand he smugged around as if his next moves were to start shaving and open some charge accounts. On the other he was touchingly solicitous of the naives in the neighborhood and with admirable discretion left their innocence intact. Somehow he sensed their need for the myth.

But I don't think he sensed ours. And in September we didn't either. Santa had been with us for well over a decade, and I think I'd forgotten what Christmas was like without him. If you added up the seven or eight years I bought the myth as a kid with the 12 or 13 I've been selling it as a grown-up, you get a staggering statistic: my S.C. Christmases have of late outnumbered my non-S.C. Christmases.

And there's not much chance of building up credits on the Santa side again unless (1) (heaven forbid) motherhood again strikes a woman who's already paid her dues or until (2) (heaven forbid) I'm a granny. Which really will only offer me a paler sort of participation in the legend as I'll be once-removed from all the logistical minutiae necessary to sustain the myth.

There were no minutiae this year. No Coke for old S.C., no carrots for Rudolph, no letter to the North Pole. Instead there were carefully itemized shopping lists offered up to the people who'd had the Visa cards all along. And for the first time these lists were not loaded with those hateful items advertised on the cartoons, guaranteed to malfunction and be junked by January. It seems when one steps into the practicality of grown-updom, one's Christmas list is suddenly void of all the "Dukes of Hazzard" gimmick garbage we loved to complain about.

This year's lists request books and turtlenecks and soccer and karate equipment. The up side, of course, is that for the first time in a decade and a half I could do Christmas without facing a cavernous Toys-R-Us and trying to work my way through all its oppressive, overwhelming options. The down side is—and this is a killer to acknowledge—I missed the damn place. Picking out the belt and boots and robe requests felt about as festive as picking out generic salt and flour and sugar at the supermarket.

Where were the whimsical wants? I hoped they wouldn't abandon whimsey just because we had to abandon Santa. So we tossed in some fanciful nonrequests to pump up the festivity quotient. That helped, as did the traditional two-day marathon of cookie baking and eggshell-ornament making my daughter attacked with a ferocity this year.

I think more than any of us she felt the absence of the cozy Santa Claus charade. She'd had the best of both worlds for years. In-the-know since the ripe age of six, she kept one foot in the camp of jaded *cognoscenti* but on behalf of her younger brother was asked to keep the other firmly entrenched on the Santa side. Hard as it is for an almost-adolescent to admit, she just hated giving up the Santa side and asked hesitantly, "Maybe we could still label some of the gift tags 'from Santa.' It's just nicer that way, Mom." There's giving up and there's giving up. And this child is keenly aware that today illusions as safe and cuddly as Santa are pretty scarce.

So Christmas this year was still Christmas, but it was a new kind of Christmas, and one we're going to have to get used to. I know that. But come this March, I'm not going to be so quick to be honest about the Easter Bunny.

JUST-YOU-WAIT-'TIL-YOU'RE-
THE- MOTHER-OF-A-TEENAGER
-:⁄:-

The thing is, you knew it was going to be a bitch. Of all the ominous omens your mother resorted to in the basic tirades that bind a mother and daughter, the one she relished and delivered with the most rancor was the just-you-wait-'til-you're-the-mother-of-a-teenager one. It apparently ranked higher than any other entry on her list of Life's Most Revolting Roles.

You, of course, dismissed her maternal maledictions as a routine revenge wish of a woman who majored in martyrdom. Just-you-waits and I-told-you-sos are pretty standard phraseology for mothers who are charter members in the Forbearance Hall of Fame.

And as a daughter of the aforementioned mother, your job in life was to limit the number of times you could be smugly I-told-you-soed. Your job was to handle with style and grace all the yuk situations your mom handled with sufferance and grimaces. Your job was to mother your daughter through the hills and valleys of adolescent angst and maintain a compassionate, uncrazed, calm, *que sera sera* state of mind. Your job was to be wise, warm, and emotionally balanced. Your job was impossible.

Impossible because no matter how well read, well prepared, and well shrunk you thought you were, no matter how many light-years of insight and awareness you'd accrued, there was nothing—repeat, nothing—that could lessen the agonizing affliction of watching your kid struggle through the standard torments of teendom. The forever immutable, regulation torments that introduce full-tilt despair, full-blown insecurity, and fully fallacious unworthiness directly into your child's emotional vocabulary.

Mainly it's the helplessness. The inability to throw your body over theirs and protect them from the wounds inflicted in the jungles of junior and senior high. Those wonderful years when existence is defined by an etched-in-stone caste system and everyone—from the most glorified to the geeks—spends a serious portion of time feeling like an untouchable. Those wonderful years when your kids come home convinced it was the worst day of their life. And it was, because they have no history of having endured the pain. They have no accumulated decades of being dumped on behind them, so they have no resilience to get them through the tragedy.

They don't even have you. Because the fact that you were once a *nouveau* dumpee too, who apparently did manage to live through it, is a pale palliative for the pain they're in. They don't care that you sat home uninvited to every single dance in high school except two girl-ask-boy ones. They don't care that you had glasses and braces and the kind of teenage skin that puts dermatologists' kids through college. They don't care that you spent an entire summer on the receiving end of a maximum of seven phone calls. They don't care because none of that helps them survive the mindless malevolence that might nail them tomorrow on the school bus or in the lunchroom.

And so, for the first time in your life, you race to the library and take out a how-to book. How to get through the next chunk of years bearing witness to the wrenching and lurching of this anguished person-in-progress. How not to be depressed because of their depression, anxious because of their anxieties, and bitchy because of their bitchiness.

And you discuss it with the world at large. Your husband says it's impossible to know real misery at 13; your shrink says it's probably kicking up some of your own unprocessed pain; your friends, who have no children older than six, say it's just one of those rites of passage, and your just-you-wait mother says . . . not a thing. There's not even a glimmer of a gloat.

This time she just cries with you over the pitiless predictability of it all. And you both figure there's nothing to do but wait it out.

SOLVING THE GREAT AMERICAN NIGHTMARE

It is nothing short of a stroke of genius. Unmitigated, brilliant, awe-inspiring genius. At last there's a way to get out of going to Great America, or any of those thronged theme amusement parks that are every adult's nightmare and every child's dream.

Dream? Obsession is more like it. At 12:01 A.M. on Memorial Day weekend, is there a child in the greater Chicago area who, triggered by some primal provocation, doesn't wake up and issue that querulous inquiry: "When are we going to Great America?"

"A year from the Second Coming" is the answer that springs immediately to mind, but heartfelt wishes coated in snottiness do not get me off the hook. This child wants a definite commitment. Even worse, this child harbors a definite sense of entitlement. And even worse than that, I harbor a visceral abhorrence of the place and a philosophical conviction that saying no guarantees me the title role when the kid does his own version of *Mommie Dearest* on the couch a few years hence.

So with teeth gritted, knuckles whitened, and Valium downed, I succumb to this Annual Outing of Awfulness. I have discovered over the years that whether this event occurs at season's demise or season's debut, its distastefulness is unaltered. Plunge into it in early June in the hopes of corking the when-are-we-going whine, and, though I have quelled the craving momentarily, it will resurface by late July. Dangle it carrotlike in front of the troops throughout the long, hot summer, and I discover that being an intimidator/procrastinator is ultimately as debilitating as a bonus ride on The Edge. And in the end, I still have to pay major bucks and put in that dreaded personal appearance at The Park.

Oh God. The Park. Surely a Fellini casting call couldn't

yield the equivalent number of middle American grotesques. And the worst part is, core patrician that I am, I still seem to fit right in, because Great America pulls everyone down to the lowest common denominator. Who would ever know that the person sweating profusely in the grape-slush-stained T-shirt and speaking in abusive tones to her squalling progeny (who wants a third turn on the Whirligig) is, outside The Park, an educated, refined, upscale specimen of humanity? Great America wreaks havoc with my inherent dignity.

Not to mention my inherent digestive system—we're not talking food here (which runs the gamut from decent to deplorable); we're talking fun 'n' games 'n' . . . rides. Clearly the person who invented those rides had his gastrointestinal system removed years ago. Even as a kid I hated those rides, but the social pressure to be an all-American daredevil was more than I could buck, given my less than top-flight ranking in the popularity pyramid. (All the worst dates of my life took place either on New Year's Eve or at Pacific Ocean Park, where I would feign rosy-cheeked delight while my innards were knotted in ashen gray despair.)

As a grown-up, I feign no more. I acknowledge my terror, I appease my nausea, and I spend the bulk of my day seated on many of the wonderfully stationary benches scattered through The Park. Lest I be accused of amusement park apathy, I do take a death-defying whirl on the laconic old carousel and spend a terrifying 20 minutes in one of the Pictorium Theater's highly inert seats watching a highly boring piece of cinema. This works out to about $7 a ride, but what price abdominal serenity?

This year, however, why not have both abdominal and emotional serenity? At the same time, I can provide summer employment for a worthy teen while providing enthusiastic companionship for the Whirligig fan. This year, why not hire a teenager for this terror-filled task? Teenagers can deal with the THRILL of it all, and all I have to deal with is the BILL for it all.

I figure when it comes to Great America, that's getting off real cheap.

THEY DON'T MAKE CLEAN SLATES
LIKE THEY USED TO

It's almost the Big Day. Back to school. Good, the shudders of relief rippling through every parent's summered-out soul. And the fierce tremors of both terror and anticipation coursing through every about-to-be-kindergartner and sophisticated senior alike. Because no matter how jaded the student claims to be, there are few nights in the year harder to fall asleep on than the Night Before School Starts.

Remember? Remember being riddled by all that trepidation—and all that hopefulness? This year is going to be different; this year is going to be better. And all of it felt incredibly plausible. That Night Before School Starts, with your crisp Black Watch plaid dress and new saddle shoes all laid out and three virginal No. 2 pencils sharpened and ready to go, you felt yourself on the brink of wondrous possibilities.

I think the clean-slatedness of it all was what made us so heady. Whether it was the intervention of three months of indolence or the regulatory rotation of teacher, desk, and locker, when that Tuesday after Labor Day came around, you always felt ipso facto expiated from the sins and stigmas of the preceding semesters. No class cliques had yet been concretized, no class geeks had been irrevocably labeled, and no academic quagmires had yet been encountered. The infinite attainability of exhilarating new beginnings suffused you.

And then came Real Life. And new beginnings were no longer a guaranteed annual event. No New Year's resolutions on January 1, no thorough housecleaning at the beginning of spring, has ever felt as cleanly fresh-start-y as that first day of school.

In fact fresh-start feelings are pretty scarce these days, and instead of being triggered by a calendar date, they tend to be triggered by some sort of drama or even disaster—lost jobs, divorce, even a death. That's what gets us talking about fresh starts when we're grown up. And who are we fooling? Those aren't fresh starts, they're starting-overs, and starting-overs are rife with emotional echoes and eternally cumbersome emotional baggage. Starting overs are laden with tears and counsel and trauma, and you never feel quite as completely purged of the past as you would if you really had a clean slate.

But next week millions of kids will feel they are starting with a clean slate. And they might not admit it, but they can't wait. Look at the beaches in late August. They're empty. These kids are bored with the beaches. And even though it's scalding out, the big ones are in the shops buying corduroys and crew necks, and the little ones are cramming the dime stores buying rulers and marking pens and going through endless deliberations over whether this year's lunch box and thermos should be thematically dedicated to GI Joe or Han Solo.

And the day notices arrive listing homeroom teachers and the all-important hour of their lunch period, every kid from seventh grade on up receives a minimum of 17 calls from last year's cronies verifying that there's still a logistical basis to continue the friendship. Then the big countdown begins— seven more days . . . six more days . . . five more days 'til school starts.

I am truly torn. Among my chronic nightmares is the one where I am back in school. And it's finals. And I haven't studied, or I can't find my locker, or I can't find the examination room. You know the one I mean. Almost every normally abnormal adult has it. So in my id of ids, I'm real glad to be out of school.

But as I see the flurry of preparations around me and feel the buoyancy and energy of back-to-school anticipations, part of me acutely longs for just one more crack at those incredibly hope-filled first-day-back feelings. Part of me would give anything to have just one more crack at a clean slate.

UNLOCKING THEIR CASSETTE STATE OF MIND

Our household had the dubious distinction of being the first on the block to own Pac-Man. And while these video bleeps are not my cup of tea, I'm not mounting the soapbox to rail against high-tech entertainment.

But I am wondering and worrying. I'm wondering just how long it will be until Pac-Man is relegated to the same musty obsolescence as the Rubik's Cubes, preppy books, and Space Invader cassettes that littered our lives only yesterday. And I'm worrying that we are raising fickle, gimmicky children who rapidly tire of the current fad, because fads are by nature short-lived, and who never find anything that will truly absorb and challenge them.

This insidious phenomenon transcends fads. For a great many of us, attention spans are brief, and interchangeability has become rampant. The little people growing up in our homes seem to perceive the world as prepackaged and popped in and out according to whim—something of a cassette state of mind.

Can we blame them? Look at their plug-in parents. Commitment and durability are rare commodities these days, as fathers and mothers break up families and switch to new ones with a frequency that staggers. The implication is not that such breakups are painless—it hasn't yet come to that—but they have certainly become commonplace. All of us are apparently potential components in somebody else's family module.

We seem to embrace newness and disposability with a frightening degree of enthusiasm and casually pick up the tidy explanations and remedies of the latest pop psychology. I have a friend who, in the last decade, has been "into" astrology, est, Silva mind control, rolfing, and, currently, biofeedback. No wonder her children seem to have an indecent tolerance for dispensability and a voracious appetite for the Next New Thing.

Our children are also taking contemporary nomadism for granted. My son, for instance, asks me when are we going to move. Not if—*when.* His closet has begun to bulge with the accumulated debris of two years, and he assumes it's time to move on to a new house and acquire some new friends. He tells me he's tired of his school and he'd like to live out West where there are cowboys. Most of all, he wants something new.

I wonder if that attitude accounts for his inability to respond to his Uncle Richie's electric trains. Richie got his first set of trains in 1941, for his fourth birthday. He kept it until college—adding to it, modifying it, enhancing it—so that its allure and capabilities and challenges grew with him. Playing with the trains demanded tenacity and creative input, which is why Richie still remains enraptured with their intricacies and subtleties. My son gazes at him in bafflement. He simply can't understand the pleasure that Richie has derived from all the years he has invested in those trains. All my son sees is a grown man watching little engines go 'round and 'round—a single-dimension diversion, ultimately boring, ultimately abandonable.

And, though my son is in second grade, his perceptions aren't much different from my friend's three-year-old who waddles in to lodge this heart-freezing complaint: "Mom, I'm bored. We need a new cassette." (A pivotal word in this child's embryonic vocabulary—*cassette*—doesn't even appear in my dictionary.)

And I can't help but be saddened that wobbly Eiffel towers won't be constructed, dismantled, and remodeled into battleships and apartment houses because my children's lack of vision and patience has made Erector sets obsolete; and I can't help but bristle on a rainy afternoon when it becomes clear that more than a half hour of "Let's play make-believe" taxes their imagination beyond its limits. So what galls me about the electronic flotsam and jetsam isn't merely that I resent my home sounding like an arcade. It's that a year from now Pac-Man will be forgotten, and what will they have to look back on that can possibly compare with Richie's trains or a friend's stamp collection?

Perhaps my despair is excessive. Perhaps it is only the ironic echo of my parents' complaints when I saw *Gone with the Wind* four days in a row. And yet I wonder. When *Gone with the Wind* played this weekend at our local library, I invited my 11-year-old daughter to reexperience it with me. She declined. Four hours exceeded her attention span and, although she didn't say so, cut into her Pac-Man time. And I wondered if she'll want to share and reexperience Pac-Man someday with her daughter. And even if she wants to, will she be able to dig it out? She'll probably have junked it in 1983 to make room for the new cassettes. By then, of course, her daughter will be able to find "cassette" in the dictionary. But I wonder if she'll be able to find "constancy."

THERE'S NO GETTING OFF THE BABY-SITTING MERRY-GO-ROUND

There is little to recommend being the parent of an almost-teenage person—except for one thing. You are, at long last, relieved of the oppressive task of baby-sitter-finding. Other than projectile vomiting, co-op play groups, and Montessori mothers, there is little more hateful than the drudgery of unearthing a sitter every time you want to make an adults-only sortie.

The availability of a baby-sitter probably does as much to determine the quality of your life as money, health, and marital happiness (not necessarily in that order).

Our friends Pam and John have all three. And yet they are

bereft. Little Missy Farqwart won't sit for them anymore because their two offspring were so inconsolable last time that Mrs. Farqwart was forced to come over as a second squadron sitter. And though Pam and John pay a reasonable $2.50 an hour, Mrs. Farqwart felt that hardly compensated her for having to leave her own premises.

And now that Missy can no longer be lured back to the house (and none of her friends can be baited either), Pam and John are in involuntary Saturday night seclusion. Their social life has screeched to a halt until they can pry loose a few leads on candidates.

No small task. Ask yourself this question. Which would you rather share: (1) your toothbrush, (2) your husband, or (3) your baby-sitter? It is doubtful any of us could check No. 3 more easily than Nos. 1 and 2. All three are pretty personal turf.

There are few sins as heinous as sitter-snatching. It happened to me once, and though I am otherwise a model of compassion and maturity, I harbor only rancor toward the kid-sitter kidnapper. Any person with a modicum of moral caliber knows there is a delicate yet precise protocol to be followed when inquiring if your friend might know the names of any sitters:

- You explain you never would ask if all other resources hadn't been exhausted.
- You grease your hard-core query with lots of soothing: "I only want the name if you're comfortable sharing it."
- You swear in blood you *never* will use this number (a) unless it's a dire emergency (such as the guaranteed surfacing of your criminal tendencies if you can't get three hours away from these children) and (b) without first confirming whether your friend has any intention of employing said sitter during the same time slot.

And with the same unshakable reverence you have for the Ten Commandments, the flag, and the Department of Motor Vehicles' "Rules of the Road," you are bound to revere the inviolate Code of Sitter Sacredness.

In addition, you will revere the unspoken Code of Sitter Supremacy. For clearly, even though this is an employer–employee relationship, you need only ask my divorced friend and mother of two, Ellen, who is at the mercy of whom. The live-in sitter has the best television in the house, the family always orders pizza with pepperoni because that's what the sitter likes, the phone is tied up every evening from seven to eight because that's when the sitter's boyfriend calls, and the sitter has saved enough money to fly off to Cancun while Ellen can't scrape together the bus fare to Ashtabula.

Then ask Pam and John why they say not a word when they return at midnight and every light in the house is on, the living room table is sticky with unfinished Cokes and Twinkies, and one of their favorite Stones albums is serving as a platter for Play-Doh pancakes. Not a word.

Because baby-sitters have you by the whatchamacallits. And for an entire decade you are humbled by obsequious behavior toward the Missy Farqwarts of the world. And suddenly it's over. Suddenly the sittee no longer needs a sitter. Suddenly the sittee becomes a sitter. And you begin to believe you are home free.

Until your little sitter calls you to come over to take care of Pam and John's squalling progeny. And then you realize that the tyranny of baby-sitting never really ends.

AN EXIT AS EXECUTED BY AN INDEPENDENT WOMAN

After years of making speeches about what an independent woman you are, it is depressing to discover that, when tested, your mettle is made of mush.

Recently I was handed a delicious writing assignment that included a two-week trip to Japan.

I got into my independent-woman state of mind, went home, and rationally explained that I would be on the other side of the world for a couple of weeks on business, that a baby-sitter had been hired, and that I was supremely convinced everything would run smoothly.

But the guilt began to stir and rumble. Guilt never dies; it just lies dormant, waiting to nail you.

In the ensuing weeks, as I prepared for departure, there was nary a neurosis that didn't take hold. Drawers were straightened, disinfected, and organized with drill-sergeant precision. Dusty piles of mending and ironing were rewashed, stitched, and pressed to perfection.

Two threadbare chairs were sent out for recovering, a child's room was repainted, and magazine subscriptions were ordered for the longest possible term.

And though I did not succumb to making casseroles, two gargantuan vats of my blue-ribbon chicken soup were simmered, skimmed, and frozen. The chicken soup was the giveaway. Somehow until I was stirring the broth, I still hadn't figured out what I was up to. But then a light of self-knowledge began to glimmer. I wasn't just organizing for a trip; I was getting things squared away for my imminent demise.

It wasn't *their* separation anxiety I was working to assuage; it was *mine*. I was going to a new country, *sans* spouse, *sans* friend, *sans* anyone who loved me. A new country where I didn't speak the language. A country so far away that the edge-of-the-earth theory seemed credible. Press passes be damned; this was a life-threatening assignment.

And here I was, spending the few weeks I had left on this planet orchestrating a grand finale of fastidiousness. That way, when my time came and my mother and mother-in-law flew in to take over, the poignancy of my tragic death could not be diminished by postmortem observations on my slovenly ways.

But the key audience I was playing to was, of course, my beloved co-residents. Because even though my farewell speeches were full of chirpy buoyancy—"Be brave and stalwart little scouts; the baby-sitter will cook your meals; Daddy will do the laundry and help with your homework; and you'll never even know I'm gone"—my real message was a tad more neurotic.

What I was really saying, with the once-squalid closets now spiffy and my individually frozen chicken soups with the oh-so-cute messages taped on top, was, "Don't you forget for one second, little darlings, that even though I've journeyed afar, no one can ever replace me, a certifiable candidate for the Career Person/Wife/Mother Hall of Fame."

That is what I would like to think. I'd like to think wife-and-motherdom haven't been too neglected by my devoting these last few years to the career-person segment. Just because I insist on being independent doesn't mean I can't insist on being indispensable too, does it?

Apparently it does. Confirmation of that was guilelessly delivered by my most ardent admirer the day I returned from Japan (miraculously alive and well). Wiping off my gushy kiss with the back of his hand, my eight-year-old looked at me and said, "We missed you, too, Mom. But Mary [the baby-sitter] is a lot more fun. She doesn't yell, she plays games with us, she bakes cookies, and she even taught us to talk Valspeak."

So, next month I'm going to China. I might as well. The drawers are still clean, and evidently everybody in the house bought the independent-woman speeches. Everybody, that is, except me.

6.

FINAL SCENES WITH GRANDMA

HOMEWARD BOUND

Grandma is going into the home. She is almost 90 and two years ago, she zipped about town in her little Chevy, played her twice weekly bridge games, and was the reigning veteran of the Monday oil painting class she'd diligently attended for the last 20 years. But now her driving license has been revoked, the remaining members of the bridge game no longer number four, and empty canvases promise only stress rather than solace.

Her body has betrayed her. It's harder to see and it's harder to hear, and the once shapely ankles of which she was so proud offer her but the shakiest of support. It is only with extreme effort that she falters forward with the aid of her detested aluminum walker. Yes, her body is a traitor and the tragedy is compounded because her mind remains essentially agile, and she is acutely aware of this corporal double-cross.

She has led a graceful life. It was filled with comfort and

travels, symphonies and parties, and many, many friends. Although widowed 30 years ago, she never lapsed into bitterness, but continued to conduct her life with quiet style. It was then that she first experimented with oil painting and a whole new world of expression and release unfolded to her.

Painting was her first voluntary step into the arena of solitude. And now it is an arena from which she cannot escape. She sits day after day in the apartment whose faded elegance no longer seems to vex her. She could hire a driver for an occasional excursion, but the cold winter air is a vise on her lungs. And anyway, just where would she go? The friends she has left are all ailing in the privacy of their own apartments, like her, able to afford the luxury of live-in help, the luxury of their own private prison.

That's how talk of "the home" began.

Loneliness can be as lethal as disease. It seems we've adopted that as our theme song, our altruistic rationalization of these last stanzas we're about to orchestrate in Grandma's life. The move will come soon. And it's such a definitive one. There is talk of breaking up the apartment and house sales. My stomach wrenches for days, Grandma cries on the phone, and I decide to fly in and spend some time with her. It is a weekend I shall always cherish.

It is not a mercy visit—a perfunctory gift of youthful companionship gratuitously donated for 48 hours. It is instead selfish and self-indulgent. I need to spend time with her. I know it will be me on the receiving end.

When I greet her I'm struck immediately by her fragility—both physical and emotional. She's in need of enormous tenderness. Evidently these last few years we've done a pretty incomplete job of reminding her she is loved. Where do I start? Why does "I love you, Gram" ring so hollow? Have we abused the words by overuse? or underuse?

The weekend goes along in verbal fits and starts. She has much she wants to share—here-and-now complaints interwoven with wafty memories of livelier times. Relating it all seems important, but very fatiguing. And when this happens, I fill in the silences with Bombeckian tales of her great-grandchildren who careen around my daily life. But I am really there to listen.

And to help out. There's one favor she wants to ask of me—some assistance in transferring birthdays and anniversaries from last year's date book into the new one. For the past 60 years these journals have been a meticulous record of the minutiae of daily living—of comings and goings, menus, tragedies, and festivities. Whenever there was a family argument as to what occurred when, the pertinent journal was dragged out and the questionable matter thereby resolved.

As the parameters of her life narrowed these last few years, the entries have become less frequent and darker in nature. May 10: Elsie died five years ago today. February 1: Johnny would have been 66. Page by page we transpose these commemorative occasions, occasions not to be celebrated, but not to be left unmarked.

On Sunday morning she asks me to fetch a small box from her dresser drawer. Laboriously she extracts from it some jaundiced and brittle sheets—four letters from my grandfather, a man I never knew well, but who is linked forever in my mind with the aromas of cigars and bitter licorice.

The letters afford me the singular pleasure of being made privy to Grandma as a girl—ancient embarrassments, hurts, anticipations. Three of them reveal a brash young man in 1910 doing his best to woo his 18-year-old sweetheart. They are filled with tender taunts—"Go to it. Florence, 'cause you're a real society lady and must come home from Cinci all in, or the girls will say you had a lemon time." The letters are crammed with chit-chat about "dandy gals," dances at the Hippodrome, "swell" picnics, and are signed (probably with trepidation) "your true friend, Arthur." The word *love* was not threadbare in 1910. One month later they were engaged.

The remaining letter was written 20 years after—his taunts were still tender, but his brashness had resurfaced and replaced the couched language of courtship. "Dear Florence. It seems like you are enjoying your convention in Washington, D.C., and that the only thing you haven't taken time to do is lay the President!"

We roar over that one and then she grows softer and fixes her eyes on some faraway time to explain that nobody ever really knew how much he loved her, because well, yes he did drink, and he did have some rough edges.

Some family members say he did in fact give her a pretty tough time, but who really knows what goes on between two people? What matter what happened? At 90 we are entitled to our myths. And, as anyone knows who's ever sought it, the truth is elusive and tends to prism off into Rashomonesque diffusion.

What is true for now is that in one week the doctor from the home will "evaluate" Gram and that soon after she'll have to go through a lifetime of memorabilia and sentiment-laden possessions and distill them into two suitcases. What is also true is that the rest will be tossed down the incinerator, or divvied up among the children, or sold off in some anonymous auction where mahogany dining tables for 12 are considered white elephants.

Haltingly she confides that bearing witness to this terribly civilized rape of her home almost makes her feel as if she is going to die twice—an urban version of those cackling village shrews ransacking the widow's home in *Zorba the Greek*. It seems important for me to explain that the dismantling of something physically does not imply the dismissal of someone emotionally. But that sounds empty and conceptual and not one bit soothing.

And of course that's the rub. There is very little I can offer her that is comforting. Reluctantly she acknowledges that the move is probably the right thing to do. She is adamant about not becoming a burden to her children, and I just as adamant in my insistence that her children want this only in order to reconnect this still viable lady to the pulse of daily living from which she is currently so isolated.

But is that what we are doing? Are we reconnecting her or simply removing her? Why do we have such difficulty incorporating our aging loved ones into our lives? Aging is the inevitable rounding off of the cycle. It is not often attractive, it is never convenient, but it is an integral part of the process.

And yet in lieu of integrating Gram, we are clearly segregating her under the guise of magnanimous mumbo-jumbo like "qualified medical supervision," "organized activities," and "individually tailored diets."

I embrace her for a moment in the hopes of imparting some solace. But how can I nurture her when I am confused about what really is right, and impotent to alter what feels so wrong? I don't want to settle for poignancy—it isn't enough.

I want to take this lovely, fragile lady and infuse her with either the vitality to escape this move or the serenity to accept it. It seems only fair that if she can't have one, she is at least entitled to the other. But Gram at this moment possesses neither.

She is simply hurt and frightened and feeling profoundly abandoned. And I wonder what makes me think I'll feel any differently 50 years from now.

It is a year later. And the odds were beaten in the gamble we made with Grandma's future. Once she settled into the home the rhythm of life began to tempt her and she plugged back in—tentatively at first, but with increasing spirit.

Her ailments have not disappeared, but they no longer dominate her. Reading is difficult, but large-print novels and biographies clutter her nightstand. And they compete with the college texts from the weekly course she is taking on Japan. Last week she called me to recommend some reading as background for an article on Japan I am writing.

When told there wasn't room to set up an easel for her oils, defeat turned to genteel defiance and she decided at years four score and eleven to attempt a new, more mercurial, but space-saving medium—watercolors. The resulting canvases are now regular sellers in the home's gift shop.

It has not been an easy year for her—she lost her only sister, she was told she has an inoperable aneurism, and yet, the woman has dug in and said no to despair.

I tease her about being the youngest and the prettiest "girl" in the home. She just laughs. So do I. At least for now, I've got my Grandma back.

WHEN A LONG-DISTANCE
LOVED ONE IS DYING

It's one of those phone calls. Your grandmother is dying. Hundreds of miles away. And she may have weeks. Or she may have hours. And your impulse is to rush in. But the family's advice is to stay home. And with their studied practicality and with their subliminal patronization, they repeat the credo every one of us hears when a long-distance loved one is suffering: stay put; there is *nothing you can do.*

How many of us 1984 children and grandchildren are separated by immense distances from the people who changed our diapers and applauded our first steps? Plenty. Just look at those reach-out-and-touch-someone commercials or check your phone bill. So when these inevitable calls of catastrophe come, you are confronted with Part 2 of one of modern life's major immobilizing dilemmas—to go or not to go.

Part 1 of one of modern life's major immobilizing dilemmas—to call you or not to call you—must first be dealt with by your relatives. Put a couple of hundred miles between you and the folks back home and, if illness or tragedy strikes, this well-meaning but perverse urge to protect you intercedes. Granted it is something of a mutual martyrdom. Mothers don't call you right away in Chicago to tell you Daddy's in a Phoenix hospital with chest pains and you don't call them right away to tell them you're having a biopsy next week on something the doctor feels could be suspicious. And all this symbiotic sheltering is done to a chorus loaded with logic: there's no point in worrying them and there's *nothing they can do.*

But *do* isn't really the issue. If I lived in the same town as my grandmother, there would be nothing I could *do* either. I'm equally helpless in town or out. The woman is 92, and her life is slipping away—so what is there to *do?* But I can *be* with her. Doesn't the *be*ing count as much as the *do*ing? If you've ever been in a hospital bed, you know very well that it does. But if you live a few area codes away from an ailing loved one, everyone urges you to be a pillar of practicality.

The relatives meant well when they said there was no reason to come in. Grandma was in no pain, she was heavily sedated, and they were sure she wouldn't even know I was there. Perhaps she wouldn't, but I would. If I wasn't going in for her, wasn't I entitled to go in for me, without being made to feel I was staging some grandstand move at high drama?

The relatives reminded me I was just in with my mom and my daughter for Mother's Day and the four generations of women spent a beyond-cherishable weekend together. Why, they inquired, would I want to superimpose over that memory the specter of this once-dignified woman stoned on drugs and shackled by catheters and intravenous devices? But was my craving for cozy Walton family remembrances so acute that I couldn't confront the grown-up fact that death comes to most of us in less than aesthetically pleasing formats?

If I'd lived in town, no one would question my presence at her deathbed. But geography has intervened—as it has between most of us and our parents and grandparents—and suddenly pragmatism rears its oh-so-reasonable head. But the pragmatic *coup de grâce* delivered by a relative was bloodless beyond belief: "A month from now Grandma will be gone and all you'll have are two trips on your VISA bill—one if you fly in now and one when you fly in for the funeral."

Horrific as the remark was, it was the one that cut through my push/pull emotions and catapulted me onto the plane. When it's time for the funeral, no one tells you to be practical or that you can't do any good. You're simply expected to go when it's too late to do anything other than pay Pyrrhic, perfunctory respects.

But this was an opportunity to be present when it counted. To mark the final days of her life. To bear witness to, and be a part of, her leave-taking, not just appear at a commemorative service after the fact. Being with her would make that leave-taking a less brutal, but more real, reality, and it was the only thing I could do that felt "right" to me at this moment and promised any assuagement.

And so the next morning I sat through the longest 70-minute plane ride of my life, gripped by terror that I wouldn't get there in time. And terror that I would. Because as needful as I felt about being with her, I was suddenly paralyzed with fear about dealing directly with death, the terribly predictable victory of it and the terribly ominous enigma of it.

But she demystified it for me. Seeing her lying on that hospital bed fettered by tubes and bags and monitors, this rather patrician woman was still remarkably refined in repose, and was still very much my gram. The eyeglasses on which she was so reliant were anchored in place and the oval nails over which she's been a bit vainglorious were still perfectly manicured and polished. And when my cousin Jeannie, who had flown in from Boston earlier, woke her to say, "Look who's here," Gram wept when she saw my face and whispered "Judy." Then, battling to connect through the haze of the morphine for a few short minutes, she was able to manage a logy but logical conversation.

Of course, most of the conversation during the weekend vigil was between Jeannie and me. Of all the children and grandchildren, we had apparently won the family's Emotional Eccentrics Award, having elected to "leave our husbands and children behind and fly in to be with a woman who wouldn't even know we were there." But we knew we were there, and we knew why—because we needed time with Grandma, time now, to hold her and hug her and tell her before the drugs took over again that she mattered and that she would be missed.

And to remember with her. The son who died seven years ago and left her asking the questions every parent asks who experiences the out-of-sequence sentiments of having to survive a child. The trip 35 years ago to an elegant Victorian resort when this then-five-year-old granddaughter, on her very first trip ever, lost a bout with carsickness and ruined all the ballgowns in the sedan's backseat. The panic and impotence she felt two years ago when she went to live at "the home," and the apartment crammed with a lifetime of possessions was dismantled and distilled into the allocated two suitcases full of belongings. And the litany of who never came to see her there. And the gratitude toward those who did.

And through all of this, waftily recalled in periodic pockets of wakefulness, she was irrefutably aware of what was happening to her. This was what dying felt like. She knew. She wasn't frightened by it or fighting back at it. She didn't feel bullied by it or bitter over it. She was only ready. And knowing that helped Jeannie and me the most. Knowing that when she reached for our hands it wasn't with terror or apprehension but with tenderness and acceptance. As if to impart some sense of serenity to those of us who would be left behind to grieve.

So that when the time came and Jeannie and I had to leave for the airport knowing we'd never see her again, the tears we shed were less of despair than of consent. Consent to the process. What made it easy to consent was that we had been able to participate in her leaving us. Just by being there together in that arid hospital room, some sort of valid, comforting coda was given to the end of a loved one's life.

So that when the call finally did come a few weeks later, there was nothing left to feel but peace. An extra trip on my VISA bill seems a small price to pay for that.

7.

MINI-
REVELATIONS
ALONG THE WAY

SUNDAYS

Only 40 more minutes until Sunday rates vanish, and you still can't get yourself to call. It's awful to feel that way about calling your mother—like being caught in some Borscht Belt comic's threadbare routine about mothers, and obligations, and guilt, and dread.

Why have Sundays always been loosely knit with dread? Ever since you can remember, you've been strung out over the chasm between the Sundays of mythology and the Sundays of reality.

Those damned Norman Rockwell paintings. Big family breakfasts, everyone bonneted and off to church, a midday roast at Grandma's, afternoons in front of the fire. But on real-life Sunday mornings, it was only the kids who woke up. And only the kids who went to Sunday school, which was unfailingly tedious. By 11, you were light-headed and gouged with hunger because no one had fixed that Rockwellian breakfast. Brunch was better. By then, the grown-ups were awake and you'd feast on exotica such as kippers and scrambled eggs with chives—albeit, not grandma and the roast. Until the Bloody Marys. Once those started, the grown-ups veered off

145

into exclusively adult conversation followed by an extended nap.

If those early Sundays weren't yet laced with dread, they were laden with disappointment and a sense of the disjointed. Dread came later.

Who doesn't remember the oppressive feeling of waking Sunday morning in a dormitory with the last three days' assignments ominously hovering over? It was a day rife with disorganization, the perfunctory call home, stops and starts, and readily embraced distractions.

Those first Sundays of your early working years showed promise. Echoes of university days were not yet so faint that the exemption from studying wasn't still delicious. What pure pleasure it was to sleep 'til some voluptuously late hour. You were on your own, with maybe a roommate or two, and lots of time to savor every section of the paper. You still had to call home but it was relatively tension-exempt and about as close to casual as it gets in the cyclical dependency-responsibility dynamics between parent and child.

Over the next few years, the calls stay superficially chatty but get subliminally stickier. You're "still" not married and there's an edge to the weekly maternal inquiry, "So what did you do last night?" The Sundays themselves wear thinner, too. The luxuriousness of sleeping late dissipates if you were home and went to bed at ten the night before. And now it's you drinking the Bloody Marys.

If and when you hook up with someone on a permanent basis, those Sundays initially can provide a lot of the sharing and snuggling that was promised on the package. But the splintering comes soon enough. For starters, there's the incessant drone of the TV glutting the air waves with whatever sport is seasonal. And for seconds, there's the wail of the family's newest addition, who doesn't seem one bit aware of Sunday.

Now when it's your turn to provide the blazing hearth, just what in fact is happening? Well, one's going to hockey practice, and one's holed up in the library because third grade requires term papers these days, and there's an acute plumbing problem confounding the master of the house.

They may not all be at home, but you're on call anyway, still imprisoned by the mythological dictums designating Sunday as family day. Suppose there is, at this time in your life, someone in your life who's not supposed to be in your life. That's his day with his family, too. And if you're divorced? Whose heart doesn't crack a little for the Sunday parent, trying to cram a week's worth of "relating" into one artificial afternoon of special events?

But they're probably the worst for your mother. Why are you putting off that call? You know she'll be home. This woman who at one time was so vivacious and active that Sunday afternoon was the only chance she had to nap, this woman has been alone now for a few years. She is still having trouble plugging back into the rhythms of life. And you feel doubly guilty because of your intolerance of her self-pity and your inability to touch her pain. Sunday for her doesn't echo with any more emptiness than any other day of the week.

And even though you complain bitterly about the consistent presence yet transforming facets of Sunday malaise, you at least have six other days—all with the potential of being terrific. Imagine a week full of Sundays.

And you pick up the phone.

LEARNING TO LIVE WITH
THE QUESTION MARKS

I marvel at the people who can deal with it. The people who can deal with uncertainty. The people who can Not Know How It's Going to Turn Out and who still can carry on. The people who know how to be *on hold* and yet they still can function. On one level I know that life is just one big question mark and nobody ever knows exactly when or from what direction the next curve ball is coming. On the other hand I like to pretend that everything has a beginning, a middle, and an end, and I'm most comfortable when the end doesn't take too long to get to. So I'm a bit dazzled by those folks who can mark time and remain sane.

People such as Elizabeth. When we were roommates in New York, Elizabeth spent 14 calendar months in what she whimsically referred to as her *French Lieutenant's Woman* phase. You remember, the 19th-century lady who stood unflinchingly out there on the end of the dock waiting for the guy to come back as promised. I can understand how during the 19th century major waiting was something of an integral part of life—boats took a long time to sail, meals took a long time to cook, birthday cards took a long time to arrive. In a world with no planes, microwaves, and express mail service, immediacy wasn't even an option.

But this was a 20th-century woman, who, like most of us, was accustomed to a modicum of instant gratification, and yet there she remained—resolutely standing on a psychological promontory wrapped in her cloak of constancy, waiting for the gentleman (who had a few things to work out at the shrink) to check back into her life on a permanent basis. Most of us probably would have turned in our capes at the end of Week 2, unable to cope with the maybe-ness of the situation. But not Elizabeth. That kind of mental balancing act required immense resources of fidelity, serenity, and security. Stupidity too, some said. But I didn't think so. And whether she got the happy or the sad ending seemed less important than the style she exhibited in getting through the middle. I admired Elizabeth enormously.

I admire anyone who can wait 'n' cope. I'd rather know the answer is *no* than be in the situation of *not know*. Jobs, for instance. Who among us wouldn't prefer the swift, painless, definitely guillotine-like *no* from the personnel department of Smedley & Farqwart to the Chinese water torture of daily treks to the mailbox over an interminable five-week we'll-get-back-to-you period? That kind of period can make you real paranoid. That kind of period can make you real pathetic. That kind of period can make you real paralyzed.

How do you stay in working order when you are waiting (1) for the ax to fall; (2) for him/her to see the light; (3) for the biopsy report to come back; (4) for the college acceptances to be mailed; (5) for the envelope, please? How do you remain undaunted when the answers to your most burning questions (Will they fire me? Will it be a boy or a girl? Will I win the election? Will they accept the bid on the house? Will you still love me tomorrow?) still remain in the eeny-meeny-miney-moe domain? The only time *not knowing* is fun is on Christmas Eve. Few of us deal gracefully with limbo.

I'd like to get better at it. I'd like to be like Elizabeth, who forged forward for 14 months in reasonable working order while the most pressing question of her life remained unresolved. So I've been trying to find out what the trick is from people who seem to deal well with big question marks. My friend John had the best answer when I asked, "How come you're so good at coping with uncertainty?"

John just looked at me blankly and said, "Is there a choice?"

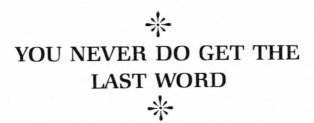

YOU NEVER DO GET THE LAST WORD

Your last will and testament. The myth is that it's the ultimate opportunity for having, once and forever, The Final Word. The hope is that it is possible to control the lives of our loved and not-so-loved ones after we've departed the here and now.

My theory is that no matter how vindictive, detailed, or willful your will, once you are a resident of the great beyond, your leverage is considerably diminished over those you've left behind. It's one of the disadvantages of dying.

That theory was recently confirmed in a major moment of mutual meanness. Playwright Tennessee Williams and his brother Dakin spent much of their lives raising sibling rivalry to new heights of hostility and nastiness. Tennessee died last year and, hoping to have the last word, cut Dakin out of his $10 million will.

Defiantly disregarding his brother's wish to be buried at sea, Dakin arranged for Tennessee to be interred in the terra firma of St. Louis, right next to Mama (about whom Tennessee had notoriously ambivalent feelings).

So who did what to whom? The foiling of one's financial desires is pretty lightweight compared to the foiling of one's eternal desires. Tennessee might have gone out under the assumption he was the one who got to say, "Gotcha." But I'd say Dakin nailed him.

I think the "gotcha" assumption was invented to make will-writing a bit more palatable. What, after all, is will-writing, but (1) a concrete confrontation with the irrefutable fact that one day we'll be checking out; (2) the inevitable awareness that others than ourselves will partake of what the lawyers loosely term our "bounty"; (3) the anal-compulsive sliver in everyone's psyche insisting that we exit with all our old scores settled.

Even if you think you have no scores to settle, the most ignoble you surfaces when you set yourself to will-writing. Repressed grudges, muffled eccentricities, and unacknowledged prejudices wormily crawl to the surface and you are face to face with the conglomerate of neurotic yechs that is you. Clearly the need to orchestrate the finances and personal entanglements of the living is one of the most neurotic. And futile.

My friends Molly and Sam realized that when it came time to select guardians for their offspring in the unlikely event of their mutual demise. Whom to choose? The ranks of grandparent/sibling/cousin possibilities featured two chronic depres-sives, three passive-aggressives, one gay rights activist, one drug dealer, and an abundance of abrasive, garden-variety jackasses.

Molly and Sam acknowledge being jackasses, too. But as Molly explained in a moment of raw rationality, "We're our kind of jackasses. We go nuts thinking about any member of our wacko family zoo raising our kids. They'd screw them up. We'll screw them up too, but nobody can screw them up *our* way."

Probably the most wonderfully fierce last-word aspirations were voiced in the homemade will of Herman Oberweiss, a crotchety old Texan who no doubt expired with his boots on. Mr. Oberweiss, short on grammar but long on grievances, minced no words: "i dont want my brother Oscar to get a god dam thing i got he is a mumser and he done me out of four dollars fourteen years since. . . . Oscar dont nothing get. Tell Adolph he can have a hundret dollars if he prove to judge Oscar dont nothing get. That dam sure fix Oscar."

One wonders. Herman may have been crafty in death, but how in the long run could he match wits with Oscar, who, even if only half as crafty, was twice as alive. I think the odds (not to mention the lawyers available for hire) are ultimately on the side of those who are breathing.

Who was it that said, "Living well is the best revenge"? Ask Dakin Williams.

THE SWEET, SWEET POWER
OF CREATIVE REVENGE

Here's a riddle. What offers exquisite satisfaction and a sense of resounding fulfillment although it is usually accom-plished fully clothed? Give up?

Revenge. Sweet, sweet revenge. There are few sentiments as acute, as consuming, and as consistently motivating as the desire to get even.

Even though we all know revenge feels good, the press it gets tends to be bad. That's because the media focus on the down side of revenge, the shoot 'em up, corrosive, harmful side. And admittedly there is plenty of that—Janis Joplin I'll-Show-Thems herself into oblivion, Jean Harris I'll-Get-Hims Dr. Tarnower into the great beyond, and herself into the slammer, etc.

But what about the flipside of revenge—the healthy, joyful, positive side that corrals our determination, imagination, and inspiration, and channels it not into the destructive domain, but into the constructive domain? Creative revenge is an unexamined feel-good phenomenon. In the interests of veering you away from vindication's more malignant manifestations and toward its more fruitful ones, here are three examples of productive vengeance.

1. Carroll was a stewardess in days of yore. Those were the days when all stewardesses were written off as *fait accompli* dipsy, and when women adopted the interests of their men in order to please. Her man's interest was chess. He was Numero Uno on the Columbia University chess team. And he harbored this grievous Pygmalion penchant to mold Carroll into a great player. Relentlessly, he'd goad her with adorable digs like "Behind that silly exterior you've got a fine mind," or "You play life like you play chess." A sweetheart. And, of course, he always trounced her.

But creative revenge was only a bookstore away. Carroll bought a book of serious, complex chess moves and devoted her whole self to mastering one highly crafty, obscure opening. Then, stipulating that if she won, she was exempt from all future games, she challenged her mentor. Heh, heh, said he. Heh, heh, said she. Of course she nailed him solidly and said *ciao* to chess forever.

2. Susan had the ill fortune to be the student of a mean-spirited, wizened old English professor who deemed her occasional cutting of class a personal affront. So vexed was he

that, despite her having received an A on all her composi-
tions, he penalized her with a C for the year. When she
mustered her courage to confront him about this injustice,
the rancorous old critter went berserk. He shook his fist and
with malevolence above and beyond the call, he strung a series of incantational hexes over her, railing, "I wish you ill
luck in school, ill luck in life, and most of all ill luck in your
career."

"Well that about sums it up," she said through a veil of
infuriating, unstemmable tears. Susan finally did stop crying.
And then she went on to do what every C English student
does whose future aspirations have been decimated by a sec-
ond-string academician—she became a famous writer.

3. Unlike Susan, Julie knew she deserved the grade she got.
It was a D. And it was in French. Mme. Hurlbut couldn't resist
drawing the linguistically limited girl aside and, with that
infuriating Parisian patronization, she heaved a great Gallic
sigh and said, "Leesen, Mlle. Zhoolie, I don't seenk ze Fran-
çais weel ever be pour vous."

Mlle. Julie took her at her word and figured one could live
a rich and full life in Brooklyn without speaking French. That
worked out well until she fell for and married—you got it—a
Frenchman. He took her to live in Paris, where she works in
the city's snobbiest bilingual school teaching the offspring of
ultrachic parents how to speak English—with the most god-
awful New Yawk accent imaginable. And dat's da trute.

FUTILITY AS A WAY OF LIFE

Admittedly, it does look a bit pathetic. It now makes five
weeks in a row that you've been out there raking up the leaves
while they are still tumbling down. The quintessential exercise in futility. But the thing is, the futility factor is a

regulation part of life, and there's really only one way to deal with it. Concede to it. Don't concentrate on it. You start focusing on the futility of it all, and not only do your leaves never get off the ground, neither do you. You start giving up. You start eating in joints that stay permanently decorated for Christmas.

Show me a person whose lawn is still littered with weeks of fallen foliage, and I'll show you a person on very shaky psychological ground, a person paralyzed by the perpetualness of it all, a person who just hasn't grasped the essential truth: Life, my darling, is one great hamster wheel. Only in the fairy tales is there a beginning, a middle, and an end. And the sooner you get a handle on that—on the resolute continuum of things—the sooner you will diminish the resentment that grips you as you doggedly slog through life's wretched little Sisyphean tasks.

Such as housework. Is there anything as relentless, as unrewarding, as futile as housework? Is there a soul among us, charged with this thankless task, who hasn't periodically gone berserk, collapsed in despair, and railed, "What's the use?" to the deities in general and the resident despoilers in particular? You've seen the responses this elicits: (1) no response or (2) "Watch out for Mom today. She must be getting her period." Under no circumstances does housework decrease or cooperation from fellow householdees increase. Under no circumstances is housework *ever* done. The futility factor takes care of that. The kids, the spouse, even your friends may abandon you, but there always will be a vacuum cleaner in your life.

There always will be a money problem, too. You want to talk hard-core hopelessness, then let's talk about futility in the financial domain. Has there ever been a time in your life where there was enough money? Have you noticed over the years that, though your income ascends, the wonderfulness of your life does not? It seems I went to more movies and ethnic dinners in the days when I was supporting a graduate-student spouse on $5,500 a year than at present, when two incomes are barely enough to keep us afloat. And no matter who brings home a raise, by the time Uncle Sam, broken toilets, and new carburetors take their toll, you're lucky to swing admission to an early-bird movie. Listen, money is the original quicksand situation. There's just no way to latch onto economic enhancement; the futility factor takes care of that.

Face it. Futility is everywhere. Step on the scale after a week of grapefruit juice and dry toast and tell me you're not face-to-face with futility. Spend $87.50 on a week's worth of groceries some Tuesday, and tell me you're not back in the checkout line two days later. Listen to someone you love make his "this year I'm *really* swearing off smoking" New Year's resolution, and then check back in with him six weeks later. Ask a teen person to turn down the volume or get off the phone and tell me that's not the definition of useless. Listen to a pastor or a politician try to resurrect some belief that there will be no more wars and that man can learn from the past, and then open your paper the next day to read about Beirut or Grenada.

So what are your options in dealing with the futility factor? There really are only two: despondence or persistence. Take your pick. You can sit in your house convinced there's absolutely no point in tackling the ongoing onslaught of leaves decaying around the premises. Or you can gracefully accept the treadmillness of this here world and persevere anyway.

Hand me my rake.

WHEN YOU FINALLY UNDERSTAND WHAT DADDY TAUGHT YOU

The thing you have to avoid when writing pieces about fathers is cheap-shot poignancy. My dad, who died seven years ago, would not take kindly to any sort of soggy prose, so I will do my best to explain this little revelation I've had on dads and daughters as unsloppily as possible. The revelation will come in a few paragraphs, but bear with me while I back into it.

These past six months, three women I know have lost their fathers. And though, at my mid-life age, this isn't unexpected, it struck me as coincidental that I had friends in Boston, Chicago, and Australia all simultaneously suffering the same wrenching sense of loss.

Of course, as I spoke to them one by one, it was strikingly evident that what was true for one daughter/dad relationship wasn't particularly applicable to another. That is somewhat curious, when you consider our mother malaises seem to shake out along pretty axiomatic lines (you know—competition, jealousy, and all the stuff we knew about even before Nancy Friday tidied them up for us).

But dads and daughters gets very convoluted. There's the fierce protectiveness of the Daddy's-little-girl syndrome, combined with our vision of Daddy as the ultimate hero, the ultimate authority, the ultimate withholder of approval, the ultimate defense against mother, and the ultimately seducible pussycat; oh, yes, it is very nuance-y territory. And Jill's story wasn't Sally's story, and Sally's story wasn't Bobbie's story. Yet, as they told their stories, there would be flashes of goofy, unqualified adoration for their daddies—which was remarkable, because two of them had fathers who checked out and divorced their moms, and the third's father never left the nest but was a blatant womanizer.

These women were clearly aware of their fathers' shortcomings, and even more aware of the less-than-wonderful deals they and their mothers had gotten. Yet if you said "Mom" to them, muffled rancor and exasperation reigned; if you said "Dad" to them, they got all dewy-eyed and compassionate. Initially I just figured Freud was right, and every little girl in the world probably does her own personal version of Electra.

But I began to realize it wasn't simply that little girls are irrevocably attached to, and smitten with, their daddies. If it were only that, then loving Daddy would be a real blind spot, and in each of their cases it would have been an indication of what the shrinks so fondly refer to as arrested development. Instead, I think loving Daddy provides most of us with a major breakthrough into adulthood.

Because—and here comes the revelation—after those early years when we think Dad is regulation remarkable, then we find out he's not, instead of staying furious or devastated or bitter (as we tend to do with mothers), we can love him anyway, imperfect being that he is.

It happened that way for me. I adored my dad because he was brash and charming and a renegade by most "Father Knows Best" standards. He careened from entrepreneurial success to disaster and occasionally checked into the safe, salaried corporate world and checked right out again, because answering to someone else always chafed his spirit. For a while he owned a car wash in Watts where other white men feared to tread; periodically he'd drop out and work as an extra in a Grade B Western. He tossed Paul Newman out of his record store 'cause "the kid was a hell raiser," and he herded cattle at a friend's ranch in Arizona when he was between engagements in the garment trade. I thought he was Gary Cooper then, but he was really only Willy Loman in cowboy boots.

I began to understand this when he was 50 years old, he hadn't worked in six months, the bravado had crumbled, and he was talking serious self-destruction. It was awful to see him in smithereens, but it was wonderful to realize that even though a grown man was vulnerable, occasionally off base, and did not have all the answers, I could forgive him and still love him unconditionally.

It was very good training for real-life womanhood.